John Wesley said, "To lead people to Christ without adequate opportunity for growth and nurture is to begat children for the murderer." Dave Arnold's book stands in the gap as an invaluable tool for times such as these.

—ROBERT TUTTLE, JR.
PROFESSOR OF WORLD CHRISTIANITY
ASBURY THEOLOGICAL SEMINARY, FLORIDA CAMPUS

I have known and appreciated the deep and rich ministry of David Arnold for well over twenty years. His God-given concepts of discipling believers is tried and proven. I heartily recommend *Discipleship Manual*.

—DAN BETZER
SENIOR PASTOR, FIRST ASSEMBLY OF GOD
FT. MYERS, FLORIDA

Christian leaders are called to transform lives, empower people, and release an army. David Arnold has done an excellent job in challenging us to raise our congregations to this level. I highly recommend this message to every now and future leader.

—TERRY NANCE
AUTHOR OF *GOD'S ARMORBEARER*

When God looked at the twenty-first century, He thought of David Arnold. Today's church needs this creative guidebook on effective leadership principles. As I read, my mind raced to countless unfulfilled, empty lives finally discovering their true place in life by finding their footing in the body. David Arnold highlights the real secret to abundant living...discipleship.

—J. STEPHEN ALESSI
PASTOR, METRO LIFE WORSHIP CENTER
MIAMI, FLORIDA

Having served as a missionary and missionary leader for over thirty years, I understand the great need of discipling believers. Pastor David Arnold has written one of the best works that I have seen on discipleship. It is a must read for all pastors and Christian workers.

—BILL STRICKLAND
MISSIONARY, HONDURAS, CENTRAL AMERICA
DIRECTOR OF CONSTRUCTION PLANNING
AND DEVELOPMENT MINISTRIES
GENERAL COUNCIL OF THE ASSEMBLIES OF GOD
SPRINGFIELD, MISSOURI

As I travel I find that there is a great need for true discipleship in the church today. This book is the answer.

—MARTHA MUNIZZI
INTERNATIONAL RECORDING ARTIST/SONGWRITER

I feel that this book will be a great asset to a pastor's library as it addresses the central issues to discipleship. This biblically based book will also assist younger pastors as they seek to establish a mature congregation. This book makes for an "easy read," yet has great nuggets of truth—then links the reader to process the information with the follow-up questions at the close of each chapter.

—REV. MARK D. ROMANO
EXECUTIVE DIRECTOR, BAY AREA TEEN CHALLENGE
TARPON SPRINGS, FLORIDA

In a day when the meaning and cost of biblical discipleship is seriously threatened by a spirit of complacency within the church, David Arnold clearly declares the necessary steps for becoming a true disciple of Christ.

—GARY C. BRADY, SENIOR PASTOR
TRINITY UNITED METHODIST CHURCH
PLANT CITY, FLORIDA

David Arnold has rendered the body of Christ an invaluable service in writing *Discipleship Manual*. This book is a tool that pastors can count on to ground their people in sound doctrine. I highly recommend this excellent book.

—DAVID GARCIA
LEAD PASTOR, GRACE WORLD OUTREACH CHURCH
BROOKSVILLE, FLORIDA

Many pastors, including myself, are constantly challenged with the discipleship of new believers, as well as seasoned saints. This book will be a blessing to pastors who want to take their people to a firm foundation in Christ Jesus. I wholeheartedly recommend *Discipleship Manual.*

—DANNY BAGGETT
SENIOR PASTOR, OCEANWAY ASSEMBLY OF GOD
JACKSONVILLE, FLORIDA

I heartily recommend this book for you personally, and for any setting, whether it be mentoring another, small group training, or new believer's classes.

—DWIGHT EDWARDS
SENIOR PASTOR, CYPRESS CATHEDRAL
WINTER HAVEN, FLORIDA

I believe the church has been guilty of answering questions that no one is asking; however, this book is the "answer to the questions that the church leaders are really asking." The students of Faith Christian University have been extremely blessed and inspired in the Bible education and preparation for ministry by this material.

—DR. C. FAITH FREDRICK
PRESIDENT, FAITH CHRISTIAN UNIVERSITY
ORLANDO, FLORIDA

I have known Dave Arnold for many years and have had the privilege of observing his life and ministry. *Discipleship Manual* is not a book of lessons he has simply taught, but, rather, lessons he has learned in the school of life. Having lived these principles, he can then preach them. The truths presented in this manual will transform the casual disciple into a committed disciple.

—ED RUSSO
VICTORIOUS LIFE CHURCH
TAMPA BAY, FLORIDA

Over and over we hear the reports, "The classes on discipleship as taught by Pastor David Arnold have changed my ministry." No church or Bible school curriculum is complete without it.

—DR. H. G. FREDRICK, JR.
CHANCELLOR, FAITH CHRISTIAN UNIVERSITY
ORLANDO, FLORIDA

David Arnold unfolds a blueprint, which will allow every part of the body of Christ to function as Christ created it to function. Pastor Arnold's teaching on discipleship will propel every body of believers to move in the power of God.

—DR. MARY STARLING
GRADUATE OF FAITH CHRISTIAN UNIVERSITY
ORLANDO, FLORIDA

This work is a clarion call to a second revolution in the church.

—PASTOR J. D. HATFIELD
RIVERSIDE CHRISTIAN FELLOWSHIP, HERNANDO, FLORIDA
GRADUATE OF FAITH CHRISTIAN UNIVERSITY
ORLANDO, FLORIDA

Pastor Arnold said discipleship is to assist in growth, to teach, mature, love,and release yourself and others to be used of God. His classes were life changing to me.

—CATHY BECK
GRADUATE, FAITH CHRISTIAN UNIVERSITY
ORLANDO, FLORIDA

DISCIPLESHIP MANUAL

DAVID ARNOLD

CREATION HOUSE

A STRANG COMPANY

DISCIPLESHIP MANUAL by David Arnold
Published by Creation House
A Strang Company
600 Rinehart Road
Lake Mary, Florida 32746
www.creationhouse.com

Author's Note: Word definitions are derived from the following sources:

Strong, James. *Strong's Exhaustive Concordance of the Bible*, Nashville, TN: Royal Publishers, 1973.

Earle, Ralph. *Word Meanings in the New Testament*. Peabody, MA: Hendrickson Publishers, 1997.

Websters' New Word Dictionary of the American Language, College Edition. New York, NY: The World Publishing Co., 1966.

Vine, W. E. *An Expository Dictionary of New Testament Words*. Westwood, NJ: Fleming H. Revell Company, 1966.

Wuest, Kenneth S. *Wuest's Word Studies From the Greek New Testament, Volumes 1,2,3*. Grand Rapids, MI: Wm. B. Eerdmans Publishing Company, 1973.

Novak, Alfons, *Hebrew Honey*, Houston, TX: Countryman Publishers, 1987.

Cover design by Terry Clifton

Copyright © 2006 by David Arnold
All rights reserved

Library of Congress Control Number: 2005932818
International Standard Book Number: 1-59185-918-2

First Edition

06 07 08 09— 987654321
Printed in the United States of America

To my wife, Linda, who is not only my constant companion, but also my soulmate and biggest supporter. Thank you for always believing in me. You are my best friend.

Acknowledgments

THANK YOU TO MY CONGREGATION at Gulf Coast Worship Center for your support and assistance in research. So many of you demonstrate the truths contained in this book.

Thank you to my son-in-law and daughter, Gary and Pamela, for your help and assistance.

Also, thanks to my son and daughter-in-law, Stephen and Vanderly, for your encouragement and to my daughter Rachel, who is just simply "proud of Dad."

Thank you to my brother-in-law, Rev. James C. Lassiter, for your invaluable advice. Also, to my two sisters, Faith and Carol, whose interest in my ministry has meant more that I can say.

Further, to my older brother, Mark, whom I looked up to for so many years.

Finally, to my mother, whose life taught me so much about walking with God.

Contents

Preface

IN THE LATE 1970s I was pastoring my first church and was not very happy. I was experiencing the common frustrations of working with people that most pastors and their spouses go through. With few exceptions, there was a lack of commitment, interest, and faithfulness. One day in prayer I said, "Lord, I do not believe that You have called me into the ministry to make me miserable!" Then the Lord spoke to me and said, "David, you are bringing much of your discontent on yourself." Needless to say, I was rather surprised. He then went on to speak to my heart, "The problem is that you and a few others in the ministry are on the front lines of spiritual battle, but you keep most of your people back in boot camp. You do not allow them to experience the heat of battle with you, and then you get frustrated when you sense that they understand neither your heart nor spiritual warfare. So start training and developing them to be on the front lines with you. Then they will understand." This started me on a journey. I did research, wrote, and trained the people in the truths contained in this book. I can honestly say that within one year most of the problems and irritations ceased, and the enjoyment of pastoring increased.

Many of the words we frequently use today, such as *convert, Christian,* and *believer,* were not commonly used by the early church. These are good descriptive terms, but they do not appear regularly in the New Testament. The word *disciple,* which we rarely use to describe a follower of Christ, is used at least 250 times in the New Testament. In His mandate to the church, Christ said, "Go therefore and make disciples of all the nations [ethnic groups]." The word for "make disciples" is *matheteuo* and is the only direct imperative found in Matthew 28:19. While it is of utmost importance to "go," we must be committed to "making," because the ultimate goal is "that your fruit should remain" (John 15:16).

Our military never really knows if a new weapon is going to function as designed until it is tested on the battlefield. It may be attractive and have great promise, but no one really knows until it is battle tested against a real enemy. The truths in this book are battle tested. They have proven their worth in more than one church and in the lives of countless numbers of people. This book is not "textbook." It is not based in theory, but it is the result of experiential truth. In other words, *it works!*

The truths contained in these pages are the result of many years of research, study, and experience. This is not all truth, but it is enough to enrich your life, and it will enable pastors to experience more joy and satisfaction in their ministries. May it be as much of a blessing and fulfillment to you as it has been to me.

Choice, Not Chance,
Determines Destiny

*When Christ calls a man, He bids him
come and die.*[1]

—DIETRICH BONHOEFFER

IN THE SIXTEENTH CENTURY, TWO brothers were
born in Noyon, France. Their last names were Calvin.
One was named Charles. He lived a wicked and immoral
life, bringing only heartache to his world. The name of the
other was John. In front of his house, where he lived and
wrote, are the words, "Here John Calvin lived and died."
These two brothers were born in the same family and were
taught the same traditions, yet their lives and legacies are
vastly different. One chose the right way, and the other
the wrong.[2] In so much of life, our choices, not chance, are
the determining factors in our destiny. In Deuteronomy
30:19, God challenges us to "choose life." The word *choose*
means to "select the best." This is what discipleship does.
It enables us to select the best, individually and corpo-
rately. By choosing discipleship, we discover its meaning,
its purposes, and its benefits.

First, what is the meaning of *discipleship*? In John 8:31–
32, our Lord said, "If you abide in My word, you are My
disciples indeed. And you shall know the truth, and the
truth shall make you free." Here, and numerous other
times, Christ spoke of discipleship. When He spoke of
a disciple, He spoke of one who is "a learner under discipline." So first of all, a disciple is a learner. It is the same

1

word He used in Matthew 28:19 when He said "make disciples." It carries many connotations, such as "to enroll as a scholar, to follow the precepts and instructions of another." It also translates as "to be a follower," or "learner," similar to being an apprentice.

A disciple is also one who is disciplined. In 1 Timothy 4:7–8, Paul speaks of believers as spiritual bodybuilders. Just as a bodybuilder has great discipline, so you must be a disciplined follower of Christ to be spiritually fit. In 2 Timothy 2:3–6 and 1 Corinthians 9:6–7, 24–27, the same apostle uses three pictures to represent believers: soldiers, athletes, and farmers. All speak of discipline and perseverance. Soldiers come under rigid training to fight battles, athletes concentrate with much intensity to be the best, and farmers must work no matter the conditions. The message is clear—be disciplined if you hope to be used of God. So a disciple means, "a learner under discipline." You learn to follow and you follow to learn.

Second, what are the purposes of discipleship? One purpose is to bring you into spiritual maturity so that you and other members of the body of Christ can be released for your own ministry. You will be assisted in discovering your gift(s) and callings in the kingdom of God so you can function where God has purposed that you should function. This gives rise to ministries born of the Holy Spirit and not of the flesh. In John 3:6 Jesus said, "That which is born of the flesh is flesh, and that which is born of the Spirit is spirit." In Romans 12:6 Paul said, "Having then gifts differing according to the grace that is given to us, let us use them..." The will of God is that you be called and not join. Being called to a particular area of service in your local church, due to the gifts God has blessed you with, provides a sense of security, confidence, and self-esteem. When you are called, you have little trouble with commitment. I have witnessed the difference. I have seen a sense of extraordinary dedication in people who are called. This applies to every department and ministry of your church. Thank God for all who are willing to fill a need, but the best path is to be called.

Another purpose of discipleship is to teach you the principles of living and functioning in God's kingdom. Many people need to understand what Jesus meant when He said, "I will build My church, and the gates of Hades shall not prevail against it" (Matt. 16:18). Our Lord was not talking about buildings when He used the term *church.* He was talking about people just like you. The church is people, born of the Spirit! Also, according to Romans 14:17, kingdom living is not a lot of rules and binding man-made traditions, but "...righteousness and peace and joy in the Holy Spirit."

Further, true discipleship will help you walk in the ways of the Lord. In Ephesians 5:1 Paul said, "Therefore be imitators of God as dear children." The word *imitators* means "to mimic," or "an actor." We are to imitate our Father. We are to imitate our Savior. Words like *dedication, consecration, sacrifice, loyalty,* and *commitment* should be positive and life giving for you, rather than negatives that you shun. In Titus 2:14 and 1 Peter 2:9, the Bible describes God's people as "special people." (The King James version says "peculiar people.") This description actually means, "private property; property which belongs exclusively to a specific person and not owned by others." This is God's claim on your life and the value He has placed on you. C.T. Studd, the famous Cambridge cricketer and missionary pioneer, wrote while still a student at Cambridge, "Only one life, 'twill soon be past; only what's done for Christ will last."[3]

When you realize the special significance God has placed on you, then loyalty and commitment become a desire of your heart. In 2 Corinthians 5:14 Paul said, "For the love of Christ compels us..." He used a word translated "compels" that means, "to constrain, to capture, to control, and to consume." Do you see the heart of a true disciple?

Discipleship will also teach you unity and proper scriptural relationship. Two ships were at war in the 1800s. During a foggy night at sea, visibility was almost zero. When they sensed each other's presence, they each opened fire and blasted each other all night. When the sun rose and the fog cleared, they realized to their chagrin that they were both flying the same flag! It is time that we in the body of Christ realize that we are all flying the same blood-stained banner of our Lord and cease blasting one another!

Also, discipleship teaches true submission. Jonathan Edwards said, "Nothing sets a person so much out of the devil's reach as humility."[4] In Ephesians 5:21 we read, "... submitting to one another in the fear of God." Submission is "humility expressed in love and service." Contentment comes from functioning in the role of a submitted servant.

The last purpose of discipleship is to release you to do the work of the ministry. As you grow in your scriptural and spiritual understanding, you demonstrate your trustworthiness to be released for service. Mark 3:14 says, "Then He appointed twelve, that they might be with Him and that He might send them out to preach." Notice that they were "with Him" (discipled) before He sent them out.

Third, there are benefits to discipleship. Jim Elliot prayed, "God deliver me from the dread asbestos of other things. Saturate me with the oil of the Spirit that I may be aflame.... Father, take my life, yea, my blood if Thou wilt, and consume it with Thine enveloping fire. I would not save it, for it is not mine to save. Have it, Lord, have it all.... Pour out my life as an oblation for the world.... Make me Thy fuel, Flame of God!"[5] This kind of commitment produces obvious benefits.

One benefit of discipleship is that it returns the church to New Testament Christianity and unifies her into an effective army. In Ephesians 4:11–12, Paul speaks of the fivefold ministry gifts from Christ to His church, "for the equipping of the saints." The word *equipping* in conversational Greek means "to prepare or to outfit an army." Paul spoke to the church at Colossae about "rejoicing to see your good order" (Col. 2:5). The word *order* means a "most precise and exact order with each one in his own place, being submitted to them that are over them in the Lord, submitted to discipline, no self-will." In Matthew 16:18, Jesus said, "I will build My church, and the gates of Hades shall not prevail against it." According to this declaration, we are called to emulate His example. We are to do our part to build ("I will build My church"), and we are to battle ("and the gates of Hades shall not prevail against it"). Paul spoke of spiritual armor and warfare in Ephesians 6:10–19, and he presented each individual member of the church as a soldier of the cross.

Another benefit of discipleship is that it brings the church into spiritual maturity by training its members, assisting them in discovering their places within the body of Christ, and releasing them to fulfill their ministries. True discipleship will never hinder you, dominate you, dictate to you, or bring you under legalistic bondage. Remember, Satan wants one of two things done with truth. He either wants us to ignore and deny it, or to abuse it and drive it to extremes. Anything done in legalism is wrong, cruel, and leads to bondage. Anything done in grace leads to freedom.

Discipleship also obeys the command of Christ. The words "go therefore" in Matthew 28:19 are literally "as you are going, make disciples," meaning "all the time." We are under divine orders to make disciples. Unless we are careful, we will do everything except what Christ said to do. It is so easy to become preoccupied with buildings, committees, programs, and so forth (as necessary as they might be) that we overlook one of the most important priorities, and that is making disciples. In the early church, discipleship was the expected norm for every believer. It was the standard for all who called themselves Christians. It was not optional.

A Sunday school teacher taught small children. After she began teaching one morning, a new little girl came in late. The teacher noticed the little girl had only one hand. The teacher thought to herself, *Oh, I hope none of the children embarrass or make fun of the new little girl for having only one hand.* As she concluded the lesson she said, "Now, class, let's put our hands together and make a church. Here's the church, and here's the steeple, open the door and see all the people." Then it struck her that she had done exactly what she hoped the class would not do. With horror she looked back to the new little girl. To the teacher's great delight, the little boy next to her had taken one of his hands and put it with the little girl's hand, and together they had built the church!

One hand alone does not clap.

—ARAB PROVERB

1. Give the definition of a disciple.

    _____

    _____

    _____

    _____

2. The purposes of discipleship are:

    _____

    _____

    _____

    _____

3. List the benefits of discipleship.

    _____

    _____

    _____

    _____

4. What are the two things Satan tries to do with truth?

    _____

    _____

    _____

Explain Ephesians 4:11–12.

_____

_____

_____

_____

The Generals Only?

*If the ministry of the church is left only to
the clergy, it's a little like fighting a battle
with only the generals.*

—AUTHOR UNKNOWN

CAN YOU IMAGINE A WAR being fought by only the generals? Neither can I, yet this is the case too often in the local fellowship. The pastor and his staff do the work of the ministry, along with a faithful few, while the majority sit on the sidelines. It is as though the ministry is being left mostly to the clergy.

A small town pastor would hurry down to the railroad station every day to watch the train go by. Some of the members of his church felt a little embarrassed for their pastor to be doing such a thing and asked him to stop. He answered firmly, "No! I do all the preaching, teach Sunday school, marry the young couples, dedicate their babies, do all the visiting, janitorial and maintenance work, run my car like a taxi, and yet, no matter what I say, I cannot get any help. I won't give up seeing the train every day. I love it. It's the only thing that passes through this town that I don't have to push!"

The apostle Paul had a vision of bringing his generation to a saving knowledge of Christ. However, he could not have done it alone. He credited the Philippians for their becoming his partners. He wrote, "Now you Philippians know also that in the beginning of the gospel, when

CHAPTER 2

9

I departed from Macedonia, no church shared with me concerning giving and receiving but you only. For even in Thessalonica you sent aid once and again for my necessities" (Phil. 4:15–16). They were willing to do their part and not leave all the battling to their general.

John Wesley stated:

> Do all the good you can,
> By all the means you can,
> In all the ways you can,
> In all the places you can,
> At all the times you can,
> To all the people you can,
> As long as ever you can.[1]

This is an attitude we need engraved on our hearts!

In Matthew 7:24–25, Jesus concluded His sermon on the mount by saying, "Therefore whoever hears these sayings of Mine, and does them, I will liken him to a wise man who built his house on the rock: and the rain descended, the floods came, and the winds blew and beat on that house; and it did not fall, for it was founded on the rock." He was giving a most basic principle of life. If anything stable and solid is to be built, it must have a firm foundation. The spiritual foundation of the church is "the Rock"—Jesus Christ and the truth of the Word of God. This presents one of the special benefits of discipleship because it gives a firm foundation to our endeavors. Remember, no building is any stronger that its foundation!

The two basic ways discipleship strengthens the local church are by developing a servant's heart and by raising up proper leadership. First of all, it teaches a servant's heart. Acts 6:1–7 describes how in the early church men were appointed to serve the people and the apostles. In Acts 2:46 all the believers were "breaking bread from house to house," meaning they were "serving one another." The need is to develop a servant's heart in God's people so that we can all be gracious servants in the kingdom of God.

The word *ministry* is a word that often speaks of servanthood. One word for ministry means "to serve as a slave, as he is in absolute subjection to his master." Another meaning is "a willingness to serve with respect and concern for the one being served." The last and most important word for ministry, and the only one that is personal in nature, is the word we translate "deacon." It means "a service given in total love," and "to provide and care for with the attitude of a shepherd for his sheep."

This kind of service gives birth to "body ministry." In 1 Corinthians 12, Paul taught that there is a single body, with many limbs and organs. The body is not one single organ but many. No organ is self-sufficient, but each needs the help of others. Every limb and each organ, functioning together, maintain health and vitality. Paul then says the same principle is true in the body of Christ. There are many limbs and organs—gifts, ministries, places of service—but one body. Each ministry needs the others, and this need is met as each member serves one another.

Another benefit of your service is that you tremendously bless your pastor. Andrew Jackson, during the War of 1812, trained selected men to be sharpshooters for the American army. They were instructed to shoot and kill the officers of the British army during the battle of New Orleans. As the sharpshooters began to kill the officers, confusion and panic overcame the British soldiers. Because the officers were being killed and wounded, there were no leaders to direct the troops. History records that Andrew Jackson won a great victory.[2]

Ministers are the leaders in our churches, and Satan has his own sharpshooters to wound and destroy pastors. With the attrition and divorce rate at an appalling level among the clergy, the need has never been greater for "serving saints" in our churches. When you serve, you learn to share your pastor's burden and vision for your church. Also, you free your pastor to give priority to what God has called him to do.

Allow me to give two examples, one from the Old Testament and one from the New Testament, which each teach the same truth. In Exodus 18:13–27, we read that Moses needed assistance. His father-in-law, Jethro, advised him to get some help for himself. He was directed to select "able men, such as fear God, men of truth" (v. 21). The word "able" means "strength," "to do valiantly," and "honesty." There were three reasons given for this:

1. So Moses would have time to pray (v. 19)

2. So Moses would be "able to endure" (v. 23)

3. So there would be peace and harmony among the people (v. 23)

The next example is found in Acts 6:1–7. The same need was found here in the early church. In verse 3, seven men were chosen "over this business," which means there was a need for others to care for the practical ministry of the church. The same three reasons are given:

1. So there would be peace and harmony among the people (v. 1)

2. So the apostles would be able to endure (v. 2)

3. So the apostles could be free to give themselves "continually to prayer and the ministry of the word" (v. 4)

When you realize that God has called you to serve and you earnestly seek to discover your gift(s) and your place of service, then your pastor can begin to do what Moses and the apostles did. The results speak for themselves: "Then the word of God spread, and the number of the disciples multiplied greatly in Jerusalem, and a great many of the priests were obedient to the faith" (Acts 6:7). The second way discipleship strengthens the local church is that it develops leaders out of the "pool of servanthood." An American was visiting a lovely city in England. He asked an elderly man, "Were there any great men born here?" He replied, "No, just babies!" Great men learn leadership over a period of time of testing and development. They must demonstrate that they have the heart of a servant. They need to show that they are willing to do what is asked of them and to do it cheerfully. In 1 Timothy 3:6, Paul said that a person in leadership cannot be "a novice." A "novice" is illustrated by a carpenter's apprentice who uses an ax for the first time. So, a leader cannot be a young convert or an immature believer. There must be time and experience in one's life before being entrusted with leadership.

In the early church, believers were "discipled," that is, they were put through the tests of time and circumstance to show what type of spirit, attitude, maturity, humility, and commitment they possessed. Remember, no one ruled without first proving a willingness to serve. General Dwight Eisenhower used to demonstrate the art of leadership with a simple piece of string. He would put it on a table and say, "PULL it, and it will follow wherever you wish. PUSH it, and it will go nowhere at all. It's just that way when it comes to leading people. They need to follow a person who is leading by example."[3]

> Christianity without the living Christ is inevitably Christianity without discipleship, and Christianity without discipleship is always Christianity without Christ.[4]
> —DIETRICH BONHOEFFER

1. List the two basic ways discipleship benefits the local church.

    _____

    _____

    _____

    _____

2. Explain the importance of serving and how it benefits your pastor.

    _____

    _____

    _____

    _____

3. Describe how leaders are developed.

    _____

    _____

    _____

    _____

A Valuable Pearl

*The message of Pentecost is God the
Father through God the Holy Spirit
displaying God the Son through a vehicle
called the church.*[1]

–B. H. CLENDENNEN

IN MATTHEW CHAPTER 13, JESUS gave a series of
parables concerning the kingdom of God. One of those
parables, found in verses 45–46, says, "Again, the kingdom
of heaven is like a merchant seeking beautiful pearls, who,
when he had found one pearl of great price, went and sold
all that he had and bought it." Some believe this parable
teaches the incomparable worth of the church. The merchant was deliberately searching for valuable pearls. He
was willing to travel far to purchase one special pearl at a
great price—everything he owned! Likewise, Christ came
from heaven, found His pearl of great price, and gave all
He had to purchase it. Paul said in Ephesians 5:25, "Christ
also loved the church and gave Himself for her." The true
church is a valuable pearl!

It has been stated that the church is the only thing
Christ said He would build and the only thing He said He
was coming back for. Since the church is of immeasurable
importance to our Lord, it is vital that we understand what
He meant by the term "church." First, the church is people. Peter stated, "But you are a chosen generation, a royal
priesthood, a holy nation, His own special people, that you

CHAPTER 3

15

may proclaim the praises of Him who called you out of darkness into His marvelous light; who once were not a people but are now the people of God, who had not obtained mercy but now have obtained mercy" (1 Pet. 2:9–10). The church is made up of people saved by the grace of God (Eph. 2:8) and who are called to live holy lives (1 Pet. 1:15–16).

Second, the members of the church are called *pilgrims*, meaning "travelers," not "settlers." They are called citizens of heaven, not earth (Phil. 3:20), ambassadors representing Christ on this earth (2 Cor. 5:20), and strangers and aliens in this world (Heb. 11:13). Third, the church is a people indwelt by the Spirit of God, thus, the body of Christ. In 1 Timothy 3:15, the church is called "the house of God." In 2 Corinthians 6:16 the church is referred to as "the temple of the living God." In the letter to the Ephesians, Paul called the church the "household of God" (Eph. 2:19), "a holy temple" (v. 21), and "a dwelling place of God in the Spirit" (v. 22).

First Corinthians 12:27 says, "Now you are the body of Christ." First Corinthians 3:16 reminds us, "Do you not know that you are the temple of God and that the Spirit of God dwells in you?" When Andrew Murray was led to write on this subject, he said with reverential awe, "I will meditate and be still until something of the glory of this overwhelming truth fall upon me, and faith begin to realize it."

When he had finished, his prayer rose up like incense: "I do now tremblingly accept this blessed truth. God the Spirit, the Holy Spirit, who is God Almighty dwells in me. O Father, reveal within me what it means, lest I sin against Thee by saying it and not living it."[2]

It is the character and behavior of God to dwell in His people. In the Old Testament God generally dwelled with His people. In the church age, He dwells within His people.

In the Old Testament, God dwelled with His people in three ways. First, He dwelled in the wilderness tabernacle. God came and manifested His presence in the holy of holies with a cloud by day and a pillar of fire by night. The cloud and pillar were not God, but a covering for God. Second, He dwelled in the temple in Jerusalem. The Bible says that at the dedication of Solomon's temple, "the glory of the LORD filled the house of God" (2 Chron. 5:14). Chapter 6 says, "Then Solomon spoke, 'The LORD said He would dwell in the dark cloud. I have surely built You an exalted house, and a place for You to dwell in forever" (2 Chron. 6:1–2). Third, He dwelled in the God-man, Jesus Christ. In John 1:1, we read, "In the beginning was the Word, and the Word was with God, and the Word was God." Then, in verse 14, John adds, "And the Word became flesh and dwelt among us, and we beheld His glory, the glory as of the only begotten of the Father, full of grace and truth." The word for *dwelt* means "tabernacled" or "boothed." He is saying that God, in Christ Jesus, took on skin. He was God's "skin-tent," a "covering" for God while on this earth. In John 14:9 Jesus said, "He who has seen Me has seen the Father." Paul himself claimed, "God was in Christ reconciling the world to Himself" (2 Cor. 5:19).

In the church age, God dwells within His people. In John 14:17, Jesus spoke of this very thing. Speaking of the person of the coming Holy Spirit, He said, "He dwells with you and will be in you." With the coming of the church age it is no longer "with you" but now "in you." The believer is now the dwelling place of God. This does not mean that we are "little gods," but that the one living God lives within us.

In 1 Corinthians 3:16, Paul uses three key words when speaking of the believer as the temple (inner sanctuary) of the Holy Spirit. He asked, "Do you not know that you are the temple of God and that the Spirit of God dwells in you?" The first word is *know*, meaning three things: "understand, acknowledge, experience." We as the church are to acknowledge, understand, and experience the Spirit dwelling in us. The second word is *temple*. Two different

Greek words are translated "temple" in the New Testament. One speaks of the whole temple area (*hieron*). The other refers to the sanctuary itself, containing the holy place and the holy of holies (*naos*). This word *naos* tells us that we are the "inner sanctuary of God." The third word is *dwells*. It is the same word used of Christ in John 1:14, meaning "to reside or inhabit." We as the collective church and as individual believers have now become the dwelling place of God. A. W. Tozer said, "An infinite God can give all of Himself to each of His children. He does not distribute Himself that each may have a part, but to each one He gives all of Himself as fully as if there were no others."[3]

In 110 occurrences in the New Testament, the Greek word for *church* always refers to people. Not once does it mean a building, but *always a people!* In Acts 7:48, Stephen said, "The Most High does not dwell in temples made with hands." Therefore, the church is not where you go, but who you are. It is not a location, an address, or a structure, but a body of related, unified, born-again people. In Colossians 1:27 Paul declared, "Christ *in you* the hope of glory" (emphasis added). Ephesians 2:22 says we are "a *dwelling place* for God in the Spirit" (emphasis added). You are just as much the church functioning in the marketplace Monday through Saturday as when standing in Sunday morning worship.

Because of who we are, we have a redemptive purpose in this earth. We are called to be "a witness." In Acts 7:44 Stephen referred to the Old Testament tabernacle as "the tabernacle of witness." It was a witness to the Israelites and the surrounding nations because God was in it, in the innermost holy place where the ark of the covenant was. It was a witness, not because of what it said or did, but because of Who was in it! In Acts 1:8, Jesus told us that the members of His church were also His "witnesses." We are His witnesses not because of what we know or because of who we are, but because of Who lives in us. He represents us in heaven before God the Father, in the place of His acceptance, but we represent Him on earth before men, the place of His rejection.

This is why missionaries have gone into areas where no light of the gospel had ever shown and have established a work for God. Since Satan is the god of this world, he had convinced the people that he was god because they knew no differently. However, when the missionary arrived, he brought the life of God with him because he was the temple of the Holy Spirit. The battle may have been intense, but eventually, because of the life of God the missionary brought in him, he prevailed.

On November 30, 1846, a Presbyterian minister, Rev. John Geddie, set sail with his wife and children to the South Pacific. The islands were known for cannibalism, wickedness, and moral degradation. The light and life of God were unknown. He arrived on one of the New Hebrides in 1848. The struggle was difficult, but he knew whom he represented. On December 14, 1872, he died and was buried on one of the islands. A tablet was placed behind the pulpit he had long preached behind with the following inscription:

> When he landed in 1848, there were no Christians, and when he left in 1872, there were no heathen.[4]

A timid faith will be intimidated by the devil, but when we know who lives in us, there is no intimidation!

> The most remarkable kind of a person on earth is the Christian. He is a son of the living God and filled with astonishing potential. While living in time he can accomplish the things of eternity. He can bring a touch of heaven to the darkness of this earth. He is a human vehicle of the transforming power of God to reach the hearts of a lost mankind.[5]
>
> —DESTINY NEWSLETTER

1. Explain in your own words how you now realize who and what the church is.

   _____

   _____

   _____

   _____

   _____

   _____

   _____

   _____

   _____

   _____

Those Who See the Invisible
Can Do the Impossible

When there is more fire in the pulpit,
there will be more steam in the pew.

—AUTHOR UNKNOWN

A YOUNG MAN WAS SEEN hitchhiking beside a super highway. He was first on one side facing one direction, and then on the other side facing in the other direction with his thumb clearly seen. He was holding a sign that read, "Going nowhere in particular and anywhere in general." This is what happens to our lives, and a congregation, when there is no clear direction from God.

According to the *Pulpit Commentary*, in the proper order of verse 17 in Acts 2, the "old men" should be listed first. This would mean that the order is: old men dream dreams, young men see visions, and sons and daughters prophesy. This is the pattern for a church to receive God's revelation and direction.

First of all, the pastor is to receive God's revelation for his congregation. A. W. Tozer said, "History will show that the church has prospered most when blessed with strong leaders and suffered the greatest decline when her leaders are weak and time serving. The sheep rarely go much further than the shepherd."[1] The words *old men* speak of leadership. It has nothing to do with age. The emphasis is on maturity and experience rather than on age. These are men called of God to oversee and lead God's people.

The Bible declares that they "shall dream dreams." This has various connotations, such as "to receive a message

21

CHAPTER 4

from God under divine inspiration," "a revelation of God, His plans and purposes," and "on the inside a divine hypnosis." This speaks of the pastor who dreams God's dreams. He has received a vision from God to his heart. This is what happened to Ezekiel. When God's people were in captivity and both the temple and Jerusalem had been destroyed, God took him in a vision back to Jerusalem. Ezekiel saw the restored temple and the river flowing out of it. Then God told him to go back and tell the people what he had seen. When God wants to speak to a church, He puts what He wants to say inside a man of God. He speaks life into the man's heart and spirit so he knows what God wants; then strength, vitality, and life come to him and his people.

The president of the Bible college I attended once said, "A vision that doesn't fade will one day be a reality." When God births a vision into the heart of the pastor, there is a truth that will become real. That truth is—if you carry a vision from God, when the enemy resists and difficulties challenge your faith, the vision from God will carry you! Hebrews 11:27 says of Moses, "By faith he forsook Egypt, not fearing the wrath of the king; for he endured as seeing Him who is invisible." The Greek word for *endured* means, "to be strong, steadfast, patient, vigor, dominion, might, power and strength." Years earlier, he had fled for fear. But Moses became strong and steadfast when he received his revelation from God to his heart. He marched back to Egypt with only a staff, donkey, and an undependable brother named Aaron. He took dominion over the greatest military power of that day, defied Pharaoh, and marched out of Egypt with more than two million people following him! Why? Because *those who see the invisible can do the impossible.*

George Mueller was a man to whom God spoke about the orphans in England and the unjust and inhumane manner in which they were being treated. By faith in God, he established orphans' houses in Bristol, feeding, clothing, educating, and loving thousands of orphans. He and his staff told God alone of their needs, never once appealing to man. His simple trust in God not only impacted thousands of orphans, a city, and a nation, but also the world of the nineteenth century. Thousands were convinced of the reality of God and the power of prayer because of the life of George Mueller. Why? Because *those who see the invisible can do the impossible.*

Think of the ministries that have been established, the great churches built, and the great victories won because God birthed His life into a consecrated follower. Why are these things accomplished for God's glory? Because *those who see the invisible can do the impossible.*

When God wants to give birth to something, He puts a revelation in the heart of one of His servants. Henry David Thoreau said, "If a man does not keep pace with his companions, perhaps it is because he hears a different drummer. Let him step to the music which he hears, however measured or far away."[2]

Next, "young men see visions." The word *vision* means "a piece of the dream" that God put into the pastor's heart. It also means, "to gaze with eyes wide-open at something remarkable." This is what brings life to a congregation—not more ideas from a persuasive personality, but a fresh word from God to your pastor.

When Alexander McClaren was called to pastor the great Baptist church in Manchester, England, he had a meeting with his church board. He said to them, "Brethren, there is one matter to settle before I accept this pastorate. Do you want my head or my feet? You can have one or the other, but not both. I can run around doing a lot of things, if want me to. However, don't expect me to have a vision nor word from God for this church and city."[3] His board and the people got the message, and they heard from God.

Leonard Ravenhill wrote, "We need preachers who are eternity-conscious."[4] This was true of Moses. Exodus 3:13–14 says, "Then Moses said to God, 'Indeed, when I come to the children of Israel and say to them, 'The God of your fathers has sent me to you,' and they say to me, 'What is His name?' what shall I say to them?' And God said to Moses, 'I AM WHO I AM.' And He said, 'Thus you shall say to the children of Israel, I AM has sent me to you.'" The word *sent* means, "to go forth to convey a message, to dispatch a courier, to propel as a dart or missile against the enemy and to emit sprouts of life." This is God's pattern. God's man is to be His spokesman, messenger, courier, missile against the enemy, and the one who brings God's life to the people!

Believe me, the godly minded will receive a true word from God, and God will drop a piece of His will and purpose in each individual heart to carry out His will. When this happens, the strength and vitality of "young men" will be bestowed on a church!

Last, "sons and daughters will prophesy." In the play "St. Joan" by Bernard Shaw, some soldiers are heard talking about Joan of Arc. One of them says, "There's something about the girl. Her words and her unflinching faith in God have put a fire in me." The senior commander replies, "Why, you are almost as mad as she is." Then the soldier passionately says, "Maybe that's what we need nowadays—mad people. See where the sane ones have landed us."[5] The word *prophesy* means, "to speak by inspiration," and "the speaking forth of the mind and counsel of God." When the leadership dreams God's dreams and the young men burn with a vision, then the people become the mouthpiece of God. Verse 18 speaks of "menservants" and "maidservants," meaning, "those who serve out of love." Ferdinand Foch said, "The most powerful weapon on earth is the human soul on fire."[6] When the church has vision and purpose, the fire in the hearts of the people is rekindled!

> The best way to revive the church is to build a fire in the pulpit.[7]
>
> —VANCE HAVNER

1. What do the words *old men* mean?

    _____

    _____

    _____

    _____

2. What does the Bible mean when it speaks of young men seeing visions?

    _____

    _____

    _____

3. What is meant by "sons and daughters shall prophesy"?

    _____

    _____

    _____

    _____

Seeing Eye to Eye
and Walking Arm in Arm

*I quit the wrecking crew and joined the
construction crew.*

—AUTHOR UNKNOWN

FOR MANY YEARS, SPECIALISTS IN aerodynamics
wondered why Canadian geese fly only in the "V" formation. Two engineers used a wind tunnel to test what
happens in a "V" formation. They discovered that each
goose, as it flaps its wings, creates an upward lift for the
goose following behind. When all the geese work together
and do their parts in the "V" formation, the whole flock
has a 71 percent greater flying range than if each bird
flew alone. So, each depends on the others to reach its
destination. Also, when a goose begins to lag behind, the
others "honk" it back in place. There is a good lesson
for us here. The church needs to fly in a spiritual "V"
formation, because it is much easier to fly with the flock
than to journey alone. Psalm 122:3 says, "Jerusalem is
built as a city that is compact together." The word *compact* presents the truth of bringing a lot of components
together and uniting them very strongly. This is God's
desire for us. He wants to fasten us together so that we
cannot be shaken and loosened from one another.

Paul wrote, "I've got my eye on the goal, where God is
beckoning us onward—to Jesus. I'm off and running, and
I'm not turning back. So let's keep focused on that goal,
those of us who want everything God has for us. If any of

you have something else in mind, something less than total commitment, God will clear your blurred vision—you'll see it yet! Now that we're on the right track, let's stay on it." (Phil. 3:13–16, THE MESSAGE). Unity and agreement are basic keys to the kingdom of God. In Matthew 18:19, Jesus said, "Again I say to you that if two of you agree on earth concerning anything that they ask, it will be done for them by My Father in heaven." In Acts 2:1 and 4:24, the Bible speaks of the church being in "one accord." An African proverb says, "If you want to go fast, go alone; if you want to go far, go together." Is there anything more forceful than unity in the church?

In Amos 9:6, we have, "He who builds His layers in the sky, and has founded His strata in the earth." The word *strata* means, "a band of troops bundled together." We cannot do the work of the kingdom alone; it takes a band of us bound together in unity. This principle is demonstrated time and again in the sports world. It takes teamwork to win championships. The late Vince Lombardi, who led the Green Bay Packers to dominance in the National Football League, said, "If you're going to play together as a team, you've got to care for one another. You got to love one another. The difference between mediocrity and greatness is the feeling these guys have for one another."[1]

Psalm 133 speaks of such unity and teaches some vital lessons. First, unity is a priority. Verse 1 opens with the word *behold*. *Behold* means "look here," meaning there is a principle to be learned so undivided attention should be given.

Second, it is "good and pleasant." Now, the opposite is true when there is disunity. In 1609, the British were fighting the French for control of the St. Lawrence River. Admiral Phipps of the British fleet was ordered to anchor outside Quebec with eleven ships. He was to wait for the landing troops before launching a joint attack on the city. When Phipps arrived early, the statues of saints on the roof of the Catholic cathedral annoyed him. For the next several days, he took the liberty of shooting the statues off the roof. When the landing forces arrived days later, he was out of cannon balls. He had used all his ammunition shooting at the saints. Much talent and time is wasted when we "shoot one another" instead of being in unity. The word *good* means four things: it is morally right, intellectually healthy, psychologically healthy, and beneficial to the family. Unity in a church raises its moral standards, increases its understanding of kingdom principles, offers a healing environment for the distressed, and contributes to strong families. *Pleasant* tells us why this is so because it means "delightful, acceptable and sweet." Is there a more delightful and sweet environment where all are accepted than an environment of unity?

The way bees work together can teach us something. The bees in the colonies are always fighting because they smell different. But when they get covered with the right pollen and nectar, they work together in peace. We need to get covered with the pollen and nectar of God's love and grace.

Third, it is a covenant relationship "for brethren to dwell together in unity." The word *dwell* means, "to mold and melt our lives into one." The pastor had succeeded in putting an elderly man asleep during his sermon. As the minister was asking for a decision in the middle of his message, he shouted, "Those who want to go to hell, stand up!" The old man, hearing only "stand up," did so. He looked around, paused with a puzzled look on his face, and said, "Preacher, I don't know what we're voting on, but it looks like you and I are the only ones for it." According to *Webster's Dictionary*, a covenant is "a binding and solemn agreement made by two or more individuals."[2] God's will is for us to be in covenant relationship. *Unity* means "we are all a part of the unity of the dream and vision for our church." Acts 2:46 speaks of the believers "simplicity of heart." This is a picture word in the Greek, referring to soil from which all the stones have been removed. Can you think of any stones that need to be removed? In 1979, the Pittsburgh Pirates won their second consecutive World Series title. The team was nicknamed "The Family" because of their close relationship. The late Willie Stargell, who was the team leader, said of this team, "We won, we lived, and we enjoyed as one. We molded together dozens of different individuals into one working force. We were products of different races, were raised in different income brackets, but in the clubhouse and on the field we were one."[3]

Fourth, unity brings God's special blessing, for Psalm 133:2 says, "It is like the precious oil upon the head." Oil is symbolic of the Holy Spirit, who brings the anointing and life of God, which results in the blessings of God.

Fifth, it begins with a vertical relationship with God. Verse 2 also declares that it comes "upon the head, running down on the beard, the beard of Aaron, running down on the edge of his garments." Twice the word *down* is used, and in verse 3 we have the word *descending.* Unity is the result of a proper relationship with the Savior. In 1 Corinthians 1:10, Paul wrote, "Now I plead with you, brethren, by the name of our Lord Jesus Christ, that you all speak the same thing, and that there be no divisions among you, but that you be perfectly joined together in the same mind and in the same judgment." The phrase "perfectly joined together" is a surgical term describing the knitting together of fractured bones or setting a dislocated joint. Injuries such as these put a strain on our physical bodies and need the attention of a medical doctor. In the same way, a fractured church needs the attention of the Great Physician.

It is very interesting to note that the word *beard* means "a seasoned spokesman." The "garments" speak of the people, for the word is not in the singular but in the plural. This is all symbolic of the pastor's leadership as he is in touch with God, receives His fresh word, and speaks truth to the people. When this is done, it is a work of the Spirit and not of the flesh, because the oil that is flowing down never touches the flesh, only the garments. God spoke the same truth to Zerubbabel: "'Not by might nor by power, but by My Spirit,' says the LORD of hosts" (Zech. 4:6).

Sixth, it ushers in the presence of Christ. Verse Psalm 133:3 says, "It is like the dew of Hermon, descending upon the mountains of Zion." The dew was the cover for the manna in the wilderness. Jesus said of Himself, "I am the living bread which came down from heaven" (John 6:51). *Zion* means, "the company of believers." When the local church is in unity, Christ can be found there.

Last, it brings life and blessing, for verse 3 in Psalm 133 concludes, "For there the LORD commanded the blessing— life forevermore." The word *life* means, "to revive, nourish up, recover, repair, restore, to be whole." *Blessing* means, "prosperity in abundance," and *forevermore* means, "continuance, perpetual, without end." This is telling us that God Himself will command His abundant favor on a people who will see eye to eye and walk arm in arm!

Several years ago in a town in West Virginia, a Pentecostal was run over and injured one of his legs in the coal mines. He was taken to a Catholic hospital where an Episcopal doctor cut off the leg. A Presbyterian woman who felt sorry for the man contacted a Dr. Phillips, who was then editor of a Congregational newspaper in Chicago. She asked him to place an advertisement in his paper, asking someone to donate a wooden leg to this Pentecostal in the Catholic hospital, whose leg had been removed by the Episcopal doctor. A Methodist woman in Peoria, Illinois, saw the advertisement in the Congregational newspaper. Her late husband, who had been a Baptist, had had a wooden leg. She telephoned the Salvation Army captain and asked him to come by and wrap up her Baptist husband's wooden leg. He took it down to the express office, where a Lutheran express manager delivered it to a Nazarene nurse. She took it over to the Catholic hospital, and when they strapped it on the Pentecostal, they said he had become a United Brethren!

Gentlemen, we must now hang together, or we shall most assuredly all hang separately.

—BENJAMIN FRANKLIN
AFTER THE SIGNING OF THE
DECLARATION OF INDEPENDENCE

1. What have you learned about the power of agreement and unity in the local church?

_____

_____

_____

_____

2. List the lessons learned about unity from Psalm 133.

_____

_____

_____

_____

_____

_____

_____

A Revolution

The first revolution came when the Scriptures were put into the hands of the people. The second revolution will come when the ministry is put into the hands of the people.

—AUTHOR UNKNOWN

IN 1328, JOHN WYCLIFFE WAS born in England, almost 200 years before the Reformation. Little did anyone know that because of this man a revolution was on the horizon. A highly educated Roman Catholic priest, he developed a strong conviction that the Bible was the authority of the Christian faith and that the Scriptures should be put into the hands of the people. In 1382, he oversaw the translation of the Bible into the English language and sent out itinerant preachers, called "Lollards," to bring the Word of God and the message of salvation through Jesus Christ to the common people. A revolution was born. Historians call him "The Morning Star of the Revolution." We need a revolution today of putting the ministry into the hands of the people.

A. W. Tozer said, "The service of the less gifted is as pure as that of the most gifted. God accepts both with equal pleasure."[1] The ground is level at the foot of the cross, and according to Scripture, every believer has been gifted of God and has something to offer. In Numbers

2:31, God said of the tribe of Dan, "They shall break camp last, with their standards." The Danites occupied the last place. They brought up the rear. Their position really did not matter though, because they were just as much a part as the tribes out front. They ate the same manna, drank the same water, followed the same cloud, and journeyed to the same Promised Land. They were just as needed and useful as any other tribe. Every position in God's kingdom has its value, duties, and necessity. In Ephesians 4:16, when he was speaking of how the church is to function in unity as does a physical body, Paul speaks of how "every joint supplies." Every member is a channel of the life of Christ, the head of the body.

Paul spoke of the same to the Corinthians, when he stated that all are important. In 1 Corinthians 12:14–25, he said:

> For in fact the body is not one member but many. If the foot should say, "Because I am not a hand, I am not of the body," is it therefore not of the body? And if the ear should say, "Because I am not an eye, I am not of the body," is it therefore not of the body? If the whole body were an eye, where would be the hearing? If the whole were hearing, where would be the smelling? But now God has set the members, each one of them, in the body just as He pleased. And if they were all one member, where would the body be? But now indeed there are many members, yet one body. And the eye cannot say to the hand, "I have no need of you;" nor again the head to the feet, "I have no need of you." No, much rather, those members of the body which seem to be weaker are necessary. And those members of the body which we think to be less honorable, on these we bestow greater honor; and our unpresentable parts have greater modesty, but our presentable parts have no need. But God composed the body, having given greater honor to that part which lacks it, that there

should be no schism in the body, but *that* the members should have the same care for one another.

No finger chose to be a finger. No person's hand chose to be a hand. In God's sovereign will He chose each finger to be a finger, and each finger functions effectively as long as it functions as a finger. This means that you are to be faithful wherever God has called you to be or wherever He has placed you. The members of a person's physical body have no problems as long as they know and fulfill their place and function. But if a person tries to walk on his hands and write with his feet, he will have problems. Likewise, problems arise with the church when feet try to be hands and eyes try to be ears. We are to function where God has placed us, in relationship to one another. I agree with Robert H. Schuller when he stated in his book *Discover Your Possibilities*, "There's a purpose for every place and every person under the sun; God has a purpose for every person in every place."[2]

When there is body ministry in the local church, there is health. As long as the parts of my physical body function as they are supposed to, I can be in good health. However, if just one part, no matter how insignificant or unnoticed it may be, decides not to function as intended, then my physical health begins to deteriorate. The same is true in the church body. Ephesians 4:16 explains it this way: "from whom the whole body, joined and knit together by what every joint supplies, according to the effective working by which every part does its share, causes growth of the body for the edifying of itself in love." Notice Paul uses the words, "every joint supplies." Literally this reads, "by the supply of every joint," as it speaks metaphorically of the members of the church. It is saying that each member of the church has something to contribute toward the spiritual health of the local church body.

When there is body ministry in the local church, there is unity and contentment. When you discover where God has placed you, you are not likely to covet someone else's place. You can say, "This is where God has placed me, and I am going to be faithful to my place and calling." In Romans 12:7, Paul says, "Or ministry, let us use it in our ministering." The word *ministry* is one of the Greek words for *servant*, representing the servant in his activity. Therefore, it refers to one who serves. The exhortation is that we are to serve where God has gifted us to serve. If we would do this and not worry about the other person, there would be much more unity and contentment!

Someone said, "Teamwork divides the effort and multiplies the effect." When there is body ministry, the purpose for Christ's fivefold gifts to the church is being obeyed. In Ephesians 4:11–16, we read that God has sent apostles, prophets, evangelists, pastors, and teachers to equip the saints for the work of the ministry. This is usually done through the ministry of the local church. When there is body ministry in the church, it is the result of commitment and dedication. David Livingstone sought out the lost of Africa with the Word of God, but he first dedicated himself. In the few remaining days of his life, he wrote in his diary, "My Jesus, my King, my Life, my All, I again dedicate my whole self to Thee."[3] This is what it takes for you to receive God's Word to your heart and to be placed where He has purposed.

In Romans 12:1–6, we find some very helpful guidance. First, we are told to "present" ourselves, meaning "to yield." We have been bought with a great price, and we do not belong to ourselves but to God (1 Cor. 6:19–20; 1 Pet. 1:17–19). Next, we must renew our minds. *Renew* speaks of "a renovation and a complete change for the better." Then, this will aid us in finding the "perfect will of God." The will of God is proved in experience and often unfolds progressively. Finally, Paul says that we must humble ourselves (v. 3).

Someone once said, "The growing Christian is like a head of wheat; the riper he grows the lower he bends his head." The reason is written this way: "For as we have many members in one body, but all the members do not have the same function, so we, being many, are one body in Christ, and individually members of one another" (vv. 4-5). In verse 6, Paul states, "Having then gifts differing according to the grace that is given to us..." The word *gifts* is *charisma*, speaking of extraordinary powers, distinguishing us as believers and enabling us to serve the church of Jesus Christ. We receive the gifts due to "grace" operating in our souls by the Holy Spirit. Any gift we have is due to the grace of God. Therefore, there is no place for boasting or feelings of superiority.

Peter adds some insight in 1 Peter 4:10 when he writes, "As each one has received a gift, minister it to one another, as good stewards of the manifold grace of God." He says, first, these gifts are for every believer—"As each one." Second, these gifts are past tense—"has received." Third, these gifts are singular, not plural—"a gift." Fourth, we are to serve one another in the gift He has blessed us with, according to His grace, to benefit the kingdom of God—"minister it to one another, as good stewards of the manifold grace of God."

During the reign of Oliver Cromwell, the British government ran out of silver coinage. Cromwell sent some of his men to the cathedral to see if they could find any silver. They came back and reported to him, "The only silver we can find is in the statues of the saints standing in the corners." Oliver Cromwell replied, "Good. We'll melt down the saints and put them into circulation!"[4] Every saint in every church needs to be melted down in the fire of dedication and put into circulation.

> It is better to train ten people to do the work of ten people, but it is harder.[5]
>
> —D. L. MOODY

1. In your own words explain 1 Corinthians 12:14–25.

    _____

    _____

    _____

    _____

2. What is your understanding now of Ephesians 4:11–16?

    _____

    _____

    _____

    _____

It Is Not What, but Who

Someone has said that a true servant of God is someone who helps another succeed.[1]
—BILLY GRAHAM, *TILL ARMAGEDDON*

A MAN WAS WALKING DOWN the street of a small town with his dog on a leash. His dog was miserable looking, flea-bitten, and dirty. A friend asked, "Where are you taking that thing?" The man replied, "I'm taking him to the dog show." They responded, "You're taking that pitiful and ugly little mutt to a dog show? Don't you realize that you will never win a prize?" "Yes, I know," he replied, "but it will give him a chance to meet a lot of mighty fine dogs!" In discipleship, it is very important to carefully select the people with whom we associate and allow to influence us.

A statement that we have all heard and been told many times says, "It's not what you know, but whom you know." In so many paths of life this has been proven to be true, but it is especially true with discipleship. For true discipleship helps others succeed. This brings us to one of the principles of discipleship, which is, *people disciple people!*

This principle has been demonstrated time and again, especially in the senior pastor/associate pastor relationship. Blessed is the young man whom God has blessed with a godly mentor! Many people who have rendered extraordinary accomplishments have done so because someone helped develop them.

CHAPTER 7

John 8:28 presents Jesus as our perfect example: "When you lift up the Son of Man, then you will know that I am He, and that I do nothing of Myself; but as My Father has taught Me, I speak these things." He is telling us here that He was discipled ("taught") by His Father. Jesus then discipled others, and it was to these that He gave the mandate to go "make disciples." Since we have already seen that the word *go* means an ongoing process, the principle is still true today. People disciple people.

It has been said, "The trees that have roots bring forth fruits." This means that people who have been discipled are disciple makers. These are people who have learned the ways of the Lord and can guide you in the right paths.

Before a person can disciple others, he must first be discipled himself. The reason for this is that you reproduce who you are, not what you say! A rebel will produce another rebel, and a submitted disciple will produce a submitted disciple. This principle is seen in the home. Most often a child will have the same attitude toward life, authority, and the church as his parents. The parents have reproduced who they are through their child!

Remember—it's not what we say but who we are, because we disciple more by our example than our speech. St. Frances said to one of his friars, "Let's go down to the village and preach to the people." So they went. They stopped and talked to several people, went door to door, played with children, and greeted passers-by. Then they turned to go home. The novice, rather puzzled, asked, "But Father, when do we preach?" St. Francis just smiled and answered, "Every step we took, every word we spoke, every action we did, has been a sermon."[2]

People are also discipled by the people placed over them in the Lord. It sounds nice to say, "Well, Jesus alone is my disciple-maker," but this is idealistic, not realistic. God's pattern is to bring people into your life to help you. These people are His instruments to correct, sharpen, and edify you. They are the kind of people who will love you and lay down their lives for you. God has brought them into your life because they have been proven to demonstrate the fruit and character of Christ. They have walked with the Lord. They will share their spiritual lives with you and help you avoid spiritual pitfalls, and raise you to a higher level of spiritual understanding and maturity. Like a leading businessman said, "The most valuable executives are those who are training others to be better that they are." Since this is true in the world of business, how much more true it is in the church world.

A word of admonishment—to reject or accept these people whom the Lord has placed over you is to reject or accept the Lord Himself. Someone has said, "Some never get started on their destiny because they cannot humble themselves to learn, grow, and change."[3] Look closely at what the Lord had to say about this:

> He who receives you receives Me, and he who receives Me receives Him who sent Me.
> —MATTHEW 10:40

> He who hears you hears Me, he who rejects you rejects Me, and he who rejects Me rejects Him who sent Me.
> —LUKE 10:16

> Most assuredly, I say to you, he who receives whomever I send receives Me, and he who receives Me receives Him who sent Me.
> —JOHN 13:20

Furthermore, we are to be mindful of and respectful of those whom the Lord has placed over us. Hebrews 13:7 says, "Remember those who rule over you, who have spoken the word of God to you, whose faith follow, considering the outcome of their conduct." The word *remember* means "to be mindful of," and the word *rule* means "to lead." We are to appreciate those who lead us into a working knowledge of the Scriptures. Never, however, allow leadership over you who is not acting in accordance with Scripture. We are to observe, consider, and imitate leadership like that described in this passage. In Hebrews 13:17, in the Amplified Bible, we have, "Obey your spiritual leaders and submit to them [continually...], for they are constantly keeping watch over your souls and guarding your spiritual welfare, as men who will have to render an account [of their trust]. [Do your part to] let them do this with gladness and not with sighing and groaning, for that would not be profitable to you [either]." We have here both an exhortation and the reason for it. The exhortation is, "Obey your spiritual leaders and submit to them [continually...]," meaning those people who are exalting Christ to you—His Lordship and deity—the ones bringing the principles of kingdom living into your life.

Then we have the reason: "For they are constantly keeping watch over your souls and guarding your spiritual welfare." (The marginal rendering of the word for "rule" as found in NKJV means, "to guide as a shepherd would lead his flock.") These people are to guide you, not dictate to you. These kind of people are the kind of people and pastors you and the church are to follow. Then we have an insight into their heart—"As men who will have to render an account [of their trust]. [Do your part to] let them do this with gladness and not with sighing and groaning, for that would not be profitable to you [either]." Guard yourself with all diligence from an attitude that says, "No one is going to tell me what to do." This is being a spiritual "lone ranger," which will only keep God's blessing off your life. If you are sincere, you will desire someone over you to teach you the ways of the Lord. Rebels only bring heartache to their pastor, and shame and destruction to themselves.

One of the basic principles of discipleship is that you must learn to accept God's authority in the church so that you can be discipled by others. In 1 Corinthians 4:16–17, Paul wrote, "Therefore I urge you, imitate me" (v. 16). Paul followed Christ and gave them the Word of God so they were to follow him as God's delegated authority. Then, in verse 17, he tells them that Timothy would "remind you of my ways in Christ." The reason Timothy could do this is because he had submitted to Paul. Paul had discipled Timothy and taught him the ways of the Lord. Now, Timothy could teach the Corinthians what the Lord had taught him through Paul. In his pastoral letter to Titus in chapter 1, verse 4, he calls Titus "a true son in our common faith." In 2 Corinthians 12:18, Paul declares that Titus would not take advantage of God's people because they both "did...walk in the same spirit" and "did...walk in the same steps." Paul had demonstrated by his life to Timothy and Titus what a true believer was, and now they could show others.

Many years ago, a faithful old Scottish pastor was confronted by his church board. They complained because only one boy had been converted and added to their church that year. Their desire was for their aged pastor to leave so someone else could come and do more for their church. However, the church board did not know of the close bond between the young boy and senior pastor. The pastor did resign, and the young boy, named Robert, told his aged pastor that he wanted to prepare for the ministry himself. Several years passed, and the pastor died. One day a missionary returned to England from Africa. He was a missionary held in high esteem by the populace, church, and government officials. In one of his visits to England, he spoke of the need in Africa. In the audience was a young Scotsman who was studying medicine. The missionary, Dr. Robert Moffatt, said, "There is a vast plain in the north where I have sometimes seen, in the setting sun, the smoke of a thousand villages where no missionary has ever been." Those words "the smoke of a thousand villages" struck the heart of the young Scotsman by the name of David Livingstone. Livingstone was reached through Moffatt, and Moffat was reached and discipled by a pastor whose name is still unknown. That pastor was successful after all because he knew the value of the principle *people disciple people.*[4]

> The fallacy of so much church activity is that in our haste to rally the crowd, we neglect to cultivate the very people who ultimately must lead them.[5]
>
> —ROBERT E. COLEMAN,
> *THE COMING WORLD REVIVAL*

1. The principle of discipleship taught in this chapter is:

    _____

    _____

    _____

    _____

2. Complete the following statement: We do not reproduce what we say, but we do reproduce in others...

    _____

    _____

    _____

    _____

3. Explain Hebrews 13:7 and 17.

    _____

    _____

    _____

4. How has the truth concerning Paul's relationship with Timothy and Titus affected you?

    _____

    _____

    _____

'Til Death Do Us Part

For the sake of each of us He laid down
His life—worth no less than the universe.
He demands of us in return our lives for
the sake of each other.[1]

—CLEMENT OF ALEXANDRIA

A COUPLE WENT TO APPLY for their marriage license. After completing the application and paying the fee, the clerk said to them, "This license is only good for thirty days." The young man, with a worried look on his face, said, "No, I don't think you understand. We want one that's 'til death us do part'!"

A dear saint of God said to me one day, "Pastor, this is my church, and I am here to stay. In fact, the only thing that can make me leave is if the church closes down, when the Lord comes, or my death. Otherwise, I'm here." She certainly proved these to be more than words over the many years.

This brings me to another principle of discipleship, and that is *relationship*. Solid relationships in the local church are some of the most valuable assets to your walk with God. And yes, our relationships with one another should be "'til death us do part'!"

Solid relationships do not just happen; they take effort. Let me give you some vital truths about establishing good relationships in the local church.

46

First, relationships take time. Good relationships are not based on a geographical location. Some people do marry the person next door, down the street, in the same city, and in the same state. But for some strong marriages this is not true. There is no guarantee a marriage will succeed just because two people grew up in the same locality. Some of the strongest marital relationships are between two people from entirely different parts of the nation, or world, even. My point is that geographical location has very little to do with it because relationships take time. This is just as true in your local church. Relationships are formed with people that God brings into your life. He knows the very people who need to be involved with you, to influence you in a spiritual way and help you reach your potential in Christ. First Corinthians 1:9 says that we "were called into the fellowship of His Son, Jesus Christ our Lord." One of the purposes of the gospel is fellowship. In Acts 2:42, we read, "And they continued steadfastly in the apostles' doctrine and fellowship, in the breaking of bread, and in prayers." John Wesley said, "The Bible knows nothing of solitary religion."[2] You need the fellowship of a church because it takes time to develop solid relationships.

Second, relationships are based on the love of God. In Romans 12:10, we are instructed to "be kindly affectionate to one another with brotherly love, in honor giving preference to one another." The words *kindly affectionate* tell us to love one another as though "bound by a family tie." "In honor giving preference to one another" means that we are to, "outdo one another in showing respect." We are members of one family, not strangers or isolated units. This is not mere human affection, but the true love of God wrought by the Holy Spirit.

Romans 5:5 says, "The love of God has been poured out in our hearts by the Holy Spirit who was given to us." In Hebrews 13:1, the Bible says, "Let brotherly love continue."

It is possible to begin in love and end in bitterness. Some of the greatest wounds on earth have been caused within church walls. In Ephesians 5:2 we read, "And walk in love, as Christ also has loved us and given Himself for us, an offering and a sacrifice to God for a sweet-smelling aroma." Henri Frederic Amiel said, "Life is short and we have never too much time for gladdening the hearts of those who are traveling the dark journey with us. Oh, be swift to love, and make haste to be kind."[3]

Song of Solomon 2:4 says, "And his banner over me was love." The word for *banner* means "standard, conspicuous," and love means "to have affection." Our affection for one another should be our standard and should be conspicuous for the world to see! A policeman stopped a motorist for speeding. As the officer approached, the driver grinned and pointed to the officer's badge. It was a tin one reading, "Space Police." The policeman's small son had swapped with his dad! The officer displayed a symbol of authority, but it was worthless. Jesus said, "By this all will know that you are My disciples, if you have love for one another" (John 13:35). Let's make sure that our love for one another is authentic.

Third, relationships are developed out of commitment. True discipleship is effective when you commit yourself to others and allow them to get close to you. The pattern for this is the family. For a family to be happy there must be an honest commitment by each member. God wants His universal church and His local church to be a family of honest people committed to each other. What is saddening, though, is that so many treat their churches more like restaurants than as families. When I go to a restaurant, I choose what I want, pay for it, and return only if I wish. There is no commitment. My family is different. No matter what is on the table, I eat it. I don't say, "I don't like what's been served. I think I'll go next door." No! I don't do that, and the reason I don't is that I am committed to my family—good, bad, financial crisis, blessing, no matter what. Yet, so many bounce from church to church looking for the perfect menu and rob themselves of the benefit of a committed church family. Sadly, so many are like the man stranded on an island for many years. Finally, as a ship sailed by he was able to get their attention. A small boat approached the island with a few sailors. They came ashore and greeted the man. After a few minutes, he was asked, "What are these three huts you have here?" He answered, "One is my house, and the other is the hut I built to be my church." They asked, "What about the other hut?" He said, "Oh, that's where I used to go to church." In Psalm 92:13–15, the Bible speaks of "those who are planted in the house of the LORD." The word *planted* speaks of those committed to their church. In Hebrew the word means, "to transplant." We have been taken from the world's crowd and transplanted into God's family (Col. 1:13). The promise in Psalm 92:13–15 is that planted people "will flourish," "bear fruit in old age," and will have a tremendous testimony of the Lord's faithfulness.

The most fruitful plants are those that are pruned, and God will use the pruning process of a committed relationship to prune us in order to make us fruitful. As long as you are distant from me I cannot step on your toes, but if you get close enough I can. The one reason some go from church to church is because they get their toes stepped on. Proverbs 27:6 says, "Faithful are the wounds of a friend." David said in Psalm 141:5, "Let the righteous strike me; it shall be a kindness. And let him rebuke me, it shall be as excellent oil; let my head not refuse it." (The word *smite* speaks of words of reproof or disapproval.) I am certainly not advocating the mistreatment of people either with cruel words or actions. But the Bible helps us discover that there is benefit in correction and reproof. Yet, I can think of people I have had to correct as their pastor. They got angry, left the church, and spread very biased reports even though I endeavored to speak the truth in love (Eph. 4:15). I would see them out in the marketplace later, and they would still give me "the cold shoulder." Usually, they had already left the other church they had gone to upon leaving us. My point is, there is growth and development in a committed relationship, and we only rob ourselves if we are always running somewhere else. John Wesley and George Whitfield were good friends in their early years of ministry. John Wesley actually began his outdoor preaching ministry because of Whitfield's encouragement. Later, they disagreed rather strongly on some doctrinal issues. Whitfield leaned more toward Calvinism and Wesley toward Arminianism. After Whitfield died, someone asked Wesley if he expected to see Whitfield in heaven. Wesley replied, "No," then explained, "George Whitfield was so bright a star in the firmament of God's glory, and will stand so near the throne, that one like me, who am less than the least, will never catch a glimpse of him."[4] Though they differed, they never lost their sense of brotherhood.

We have both a vertical relationship with God and a horizontal relationship with one another. According to Ephesians 4:15–16, we receive strength and support from Christ our head and from one another in our local church family. This is why our relationships should be "'til death do us part.'"

Some birds once decided to form their own church, so they called an organizational meeting. The duck stood up and said, "I'm for water baptism by immersion. It's the only sure way to get their wallets wet." The rooster replied, "No, I don't agree. We should baptize by sprinkling so as to not embarrass anyone." The parrot objected that baptism was not the most important thing, but rather good programs. Several of the birds cheered loudly, because they wanted programs, too. The mockingbird spoke up, "What about the choir and the organ?" "Oh," said the sparrow, "we don't need an organ." The redbird did not want any instruments at all, and the hawk wanted to do away with music altogether. The goose stood and said, "We need a pastor who is good with the young people." The blue jay figured that as long as the preacher would agree not to preach against sin and stuff like that, almost any minister would do, because he would be popular in the community. Then the wise owl expressed, "Brethren, all these things are secondary. What we need is sincerity." "Yes sir," he repeated, quite pleased with himself. "Above all else we must be real and sincere, even if we don't mean it." And so they formed a church, and it was certainly for the birds!

> An experience of God that costs nothing is worth nothing and does nothing.[5]
>
> —LEONARD RAVENHILL

1. List the three things that form relationships.

   _____

   _____

   _____

   _____

2. How does the comparison of a restaurant to your church affect you?

   _____

   _____

   _____

   _____

3. Explain what you learned from Psalm 92:13–15.

   _____

   _____

   _____

   _____

A Vertical Relationship

*God created the world out of nothing and
as long as we are nothing, God can make
something out of us.*[1]

—MARTIN LUTHER

ARTURO TOSCANINI, A RENOWNED conductor at
the Metropolitan Opera House in New York City, offered
a featured soloist some constructive criticism during a
rehearsal. The soloist, who was too obstinate to accept his
suggestions, retorted, "I am the star of this performance."
Toscanini replied, "Madame, in this performance there
are no stars."[2]

This brings me to a third principle of discipleship,
which is *submission*. Discipleship cannot be successful
unless we are submitted, because only the submitted can
be trained. When we are submitted we acknowledge our
need of training and development. A rebel is one who
mistakenly believes he can make it on his own. However,
when we submit to discipleship we demonstrate a major
step in the development of our character.

A word of caution—even though submission is necessary, it can also be dangerous. Unqualified submission
that lacks the necessary qualifications and is not limited or
modified is both unwise and unscriptural. I believe the best
definition I've heard of submission is "humility expressed
in love and service." So, that which is imposed is legalism
and controlling, and has no place within the body of Christ.

CHAPTER 9

Submission is a voluntary choice and decision.

One reason submission is necessary is because of the spirit of this age. In Matthew 24:12, Jesus gave one of the signs of the last days when He stated, "And because lawlessness will abound, the love of many will grow cold." He is describing the spirit of this age. The word *lawlessness* speaks of a generation that is selfish, self-centered, rebellious, and does only what serves its best interests. The word *love* is the *agape* love of John 3:16. Our Lord is saying that in the last days people will care for themselves and have very little regard for others. John made a statement that is most revealing and deeply concerning when he wrote, "And this is the spirit of the Antichrist, which you have heard was coming, and is now already in the world" (1 John 4:3). The spirit of Antichrist is a spirit of rebellion, the same rebellion Jesus spoke of in Matthew 24:12. According to Scripture, the spirit of rebellion is already in the world. If it was true over 2,000 years ago, how much more so today!

Submission begins with our vertical relationship and obedience to Christ. There are two kingdoms operating in this world today. First, there is the kingdom of Jesus Christ, which is a spirit of submission. Second, there is the kingdom of Satan, which is a spirit of rebellion. Let's take a closer look at both so as to discover how they can influence our lives.

First of all, we have the kingdom of Jesus Christ, whose attitude is the essence of His kingdom. In Matthew 26:39, Jesus demonstrated His submission to His Father in the garden: "He went a little farther and fell on His face, and prayed, saying, 'O My Father, if it is possible, let this cup pass from Me; nevertheless, not as I will, but as You will.'"

Look with me further at Philippians 2:1–11. Here the Bible gives one of the major causes for disunity and discord in the church. Paul begins by making his plea for love, fellowship, and unity in verses 1 and 2. Then, in the first half of verse 3 he speaks of "selfish ambition." This speaks of a person whose concentration is on self and personal prestige. He is concerned, first and foremost, with his self-interest. The object of his life is not to honor, help, and edify others, but to push and put them down. The word *selfish* speaks of "contentions" and "arrogance." Then, Paul returns to his plea in verses 3 and 4 by repeating it, and then giving the supreme example for us to follow in verses 5–11, which is our Lord. In verse 5, the "mind" means "this attitude of Jesus Christ." And what is the attitude we are to have? It is the same as Christ had that made Him take seven steps down in submission, to die the death of the cross (vv. 5–8). Then, there were seven ways His Father exalted Him (vv. 9–11).

No one experienced submission any more that Jesus did. He was equal with God, yet He was willing to submit and die the death of the cross. Because He was willing to submit, the Bible says, "Therefore God also has highly exalted Him and given Him the name which is above every name" (v. 9). Jesus Christ was the incarnation of God. He declared the glory of God. He was the express image of the Father. Yet, He humbled Himself. A Christmas card illustrates the attitude of Christ. On the front of the card is an array of dictators, world leaders, and kings throughout history, men such as Julius Caesar, Napoleon, Alexander the Great, Lenin, and Hitler. The words on the front of the card said: "History is crowded with men who would be gods." Then, on the inside are the words: "But only one God who would be man." First John 2:6 advises, "He who says he abides in Him ought himself also to walk just as He walked."

In Ephesians 5:18–21, we discover that the nature of spirituality is submission, and not the "gifts." We are spiritual to the degree we are willing to submit. The lesson for us is this: If we will humble ourselves and submit, God will exalt us, but if we exalt ourselves, God will humble us.

A man from the Midwest was visiting his brother in Hollywood, California. The California brother suggested they have dinner and invited along a "would-be-movie-actor" to join them. As they sat at the table, the aspiring actor boasted quite regularly of his accomplishments. They also noticed that the waitress kept eyeing him. Finally, she approached and asked, "Haven't I seen you somewhere before?" Trying to appear modest, the actor said, "Perhaps you've seen me in the movies." She replied, "Could be. Where do you usually sit?"

Second, we have the kingdom of Satan, whose attitude is the essence of his kingdom. In Isaiah 14:12–17, we have the record of Satan's rebellion and fall. He said, "I will be like the Most High" (v. 14). The phrase "Most High" is a title to speak of God's ultimate authority. It also speaks of His absolute right to rule. Satan, in essence, was saying, "You'll not rule over me. I'm not going to take Your commands, follow You, or obey You." His attitude was the exact opposite of Christ's. In the garden, Jesus said, "Not My will." Yet, five times here in Isaiah, Satan said "I will" in just two verses (13–14)! The lesson for us is this: Each of us must realize that we were born with a rebel nature that says "my will, my way, please myself." The cross of Jesus Christ must be applied to that rebel nature that is in rebellion against submission.

A little boy was antagonizing his mother, so she told him to sit down. He replied, "No!" She looked at him, and with additional firmness, repeated, "Sit down!" He again replied, "No!" Walking over to him, she grabbed him by the shoulders and, pushing him down onto the chair, said, "Now you'll sit down!" Looking up at his mother, he remarked, "I may be sitting down on the outside, but I'm standing up in the inside!" Sadly, I have seen this attitude demonstrated over and over again. A person looks and acts spiritual until their submission is tested; then you discover what they are really like on the inside!

In Psalm 37:35, David wrote, "I have seen the wicked in great power, and spreading himself like a native green tree." The "native green tree" he speaks of is a tree that dies inside while it continues to grow and enlarge itself on the outside.

However, one day its internal weakness will no longer support its size, and it falls. What is true of this tree can be true of a congregation and a person.

In 1 Samuel 15:23, Samuel said to Saul, "For rebellion is as the sin of witchcraft, and stubbornness is as iniquity and idolatry. Because you have rejected the word of the LORD, He also has rejected you from being king." In verse 26, Samuel reiterated the same, "But Samuel said to Saul, 'I will not return with you, for you have rejected the word of the LORD, and the LORD has rejected you from being king over Israel.'" In the following chapter, the Bible records, "Now the LORD said to Samuel, 'How long will you mourn for Saul, seeing I have rejected him from reigning over Israel?'" The word for *rebellion* used in these verses pertaining to Saul's rebellion means, "to spurn, disappear, abhor, despise, melt away, reprobate and to loathe." Four times in these references the word *rejected* is used. Because Saul spurned, abhorred, despised, and loathed obeying God, it led to his reprobate ways, and he melted away and disappeared! I trust you have seen that rebellion is no laughing matter. I have witnessed more than one person, whether they stood in the pulpit or sat in the pew, render themselves ineffective for service in God's kingdom because of a rebellious attitude.

After Thorvaldsen had completed his famous statue of Christ, he brought one of his friends to view it. Christ's arms were outstretched, His head bowed between them. Thorvalden's friend said, "But I cannot see His face." The artist replied, "If you would see the face of Christ you must get on your knees."[2] We must humble ourselves before Him if we are to be discipled. Remember, submission is not what we say, but it is an attitude and an act.

> You cannot make Christ the King of your life until you abdicate.
>
> —AUTHOR UNKNOWN

1. What is the message you received from Christ's words in Matthew 24:12?

_____

_____

_____

_____

2. What are the two kingdoms operating in the world today?

_____

_____

_____

_____

3. What have you learned about rebellion?

_____

_____

_____

_____

Horizontal Results

*It's easy to halve the potato where there
is love.*

—IRISH PROVERB

MOST EVERYONE WAS CONVINCED HE was going
the wrong way. In a NCAA 10,000-meter cross-country
race in Riverside, California, 123 of the 127 competitors
thought Mike Delcavo was going in the wrong direction.
He kept waving for them to follow him, but only four
believed he had taken the proper turn. It was the turn that
all the other runners had missed. When he was questioned
about his choice of direction and how he did not allow
the crowds reaction to deter him, he responded, "They
thought it was funny that I went the right way."[1] If you
choose the way of submission, it will be the opposite of
society's mind-set, but it will be the right way.

We have both a vertical relationship with God and a
horizontal relationship with one another. God taught this
in how He arranged the Ten Commandments. The first
four speak of our vertical relationship with God, and the
following six speak of our horizontal relationship with one
another. This truth is contained throughout Scripture. In
other words, if we get things right with God, things will
go much smoother in our contact with each other. It is
the same with submission. When we submit to God, as
I spoke of in the previous chapter, we then can submit to
one another.

CHAPTER 10

The Bible teaches seven areas of submission in life. In every case Scripture addresses the one who is to submit. The first is human government. In Romans 13:1–5, Paul addresses this very subject. Second, we are to submit to one another. Ephesians 5:21 says, "Submitting to one another in the fear of God." We cannot treat God one way and treat our spouse, pastor, or a fellow believer some other way. Our relationship with the Lord is reflected in our relationship with people. Third, husbands and wives are to submit to each other (Eph. 5:21–33). Fourth, children are to submit to their parents (Eph. 6:1–3). Fifth, employees are to submit to their employers (Eph. 6:5–8). Sixth, believers are to submit to their elders (Heb. 13:7, 17). Seventh, the younger are to submit to the elders (1 Pet. 5:5).

There is also God's human delegated authority to which we are to show submission. Blaise Pascal, the brilliant seventeenth-century French mathematician and philosopher, was converted to Christ. He had what he termed a powerful born-again experience. Soon thereafter, he wrote these words, "Total submission to Jesus Christ and my director."[2] Pascal was a member of the Roman Catholic Jansenist sect. His director was the man the sect placed over him as his spiritual mentor. This is a rather remarkable attitude, considering Blaise Pascal was the discoverer of calculus and barometric pressure and a most profound author. Although his mentor was certainly inferior to him intellectually, Pascal submitted to him as a practical submission to Jesus Christ. He could not conceive of submission to the Lord without some kind of submission to God's human delegated authority. In His mandate found in Matthew 28:18–20, Christ sent out His delegated authority, and still does so today. However, it is His authority given to us, and apart from Him we have no authority. Christ Jesus still has His human delegated authority in the church today. It is His authority, but He directs and rules through human beings to whom He has given that authority! This is why we are to show respect and submission to those whom Christ has endowed with His authority. We cannot treat Christ one way and treat His delegated authority another way. Hebrews 13:7, 17, and 24 teach that we are to show respect to those whom God has placed over us.

We are also expected to submit to one another. A rather prominent sports figure attended a black-tie banquet with more than a thousand in attendance. He was seated at the head table with other dignitaries. He realized he did not have enough butter for his meal. He motioned to the waiter and demanded additional butter. The waiter replied, "I'm sorry, but we can only give one pat of butter to each person." The man said to the waiter, "I don't believe you know who I am. I'm the guest speaker tonight and a celebrity in the sports world. I've participated in some of the largest events, including Super Bowls." The waiter answered, "I guess you don't know who I am." The speaker answered, "No, I guess not." The waiter said with confidence, "I am the man in charge of the butter." We all have someone to submit to.

In 1 John 4:20–21 we read, "If someone says, 'I love God,' and hates his brother, he is a liar; for he who does not love his brother whom he has seen, how can he love God whom he has not seen? And this commandment we have from Him: that he who loves God must love his brother also." You cannot treat Jesus Christ one way and treat your brother or sister another way. You cannot be on speaking terms with God and not be on speaking terms with one another. You cannot be right with God and have something in your heart against your spouse, parents, or fellow Christians. You cannot be vocal with God and give others the silent treatment. Remember, your relationship with others reflects your relationship with the Lord.

In 1 Peter 5:5–6, we see the same truth: "Likewise, you younger people, submit yourselves to your elders. Yes, all of you be submissive to one another, and be clothed with humility, for 'God resists the proud but gives grace to the humble.' Therefore, humble yourselves under the mighty hand of God, that He may exalt you in due time." During my years in the church, I've heard a lot more about verse 6 than verse 5. One reason is that it looks and sounds spiritual to bow and weep before God. Also, it's easier. In verse 5, though, God is saying, "Submission and humility are not only an attitude toward God, but also toward one another." The lesson to be learned here is that there is no way to humble yourself before God without humbling yourself before one another. We humble ourselves before the Lord by humbling ourselves before the Lord's people.

The principles of submission: First, no one is qualified to lead until they first learn to serve. Never submit to someone who is not under some kind of biblical authority themselves. John Calvin said, "We are subject to those who rule over us, but subject only in the Lord. If they command anything against Him, let us not pay the least regard to it."[3] Anyone who has people submitted to his leadership must be under submission. In Luke 22:24–27, Jesus taught that the leader is to become a servant, for the one willing to be a servant will be a leader.

Second, submission is not only taught, but caught. We reproduce who we are, not what we say.

Third, the essence of spirituality is submission. As contrary as it seems to misguided perception, true spirituality is not spiritual gifts, talents, preaching, singing, or many other worthy things. It is possible for God to work through someone who does not allow the Lord to work in him! In Ephesians 5:18–6:9, Paul is describing a lifestyle out in the marketplace. To put it quite simply, he reminds us that if the Spirit-filled life does not work practically, it does not work at all. The true Spirit-filled life must work at home, on the job, in the marriage, in the family, and throughout the week.

Fourth, submission is not forced; it is a decision. In Matthew 20:25–28, Christ said that submission to civil authority is forced, like an officer making a person obey the law, but submission in the Bible is volitional, a decision. You and I make decisions throughout the day to either be submissive or nonsubmissive. Either choice is a decision from the heart.

Fifth, submission is the method God uses to deal with pride. It has been said that pride was the ingredient in the sin that turned angels into demons. One scriptural definition of pride means, "one who shows himself above other people." In the Greek of the original New Testament, the word for *I* was *ego.* Today we use it to describe someone who has an inflated opinion of himself. Peter said, "God resists the proud, but gives grace to the humble" (1 Pet. 5:5). The Greek word for *resists* means, "to battle against, to oppose, or to foil the plans of someone." Success can either develop us or destroy us. This is why Peter first said, "All of you be submissive to one another, and be clothed with humility." Remember, it is as one said: "Conceit is the devil's gift to little men!"

A wristwatch became bored with his lowly position and desired to be the big clock on the front of a large government building. One day someone gave him what he wished for. It was hoisted to the top of the tall building, appearing smaller and smaller to those watching from below. When the wristwatch arrived at the top, those watching from the ground could no longer see it. Its elevation had become its annihilation! Peter Marshall prayed, "When I am wrong, dear Lord, make me easy to change, and when I am right, make me easy to live with."[4]

In Proverbs 16:18–19 Solomon wrote, "Pride goes before destruction, and a haughty spirit before a fall. Better to be of a humble spirit with the lowly, than to divide the spoil with the proud." One of the root meanings of *humility* is "a package" or "a bundle." When we humble ourselves before

63

God and man, we can become "quite a package" for God to use.

Sixth, submission is God's method of promotion. Jesus said, "And whoever exalts himself will be humbled, and he who humbles himself will be exalted" (Matt. 23:12).

Seventh, submission is the way to fruitfulness. Again, Christ addressed this subject when He said, "Most assuredly, I say to you, unless a grain of wheat falls into the ground and dies, it remains alone; but if it dies, it produces much grain" (John 12:24).

Charles Haddon Spurgeon told a story about William Carey, the Baptist minister and missionary to India. When Carey was dangerously ill, someone asked him, "If this sickness proves fatal, what passage would you select as the text for your funeral sermon?" He answered, "Oh, I feel that such a poor sinful creature is unworthy to have anything said about him; but if a funeral sermon must be preached, let it be from the words, 'Have mercy upon me, O God, according to Thy lovingkindness, according unto the multitude of Thy tender mercies blot out my transgressions.'" In his will he directed to have the following inscription and nothing more engraved on his gravestone:[5]

> William Carey
> Born August 17, 1761
> Died _____
> A wretched, poor, and helpless worm
> On Thy kind arms I fall.

In our modern church culture, we may declare this to be too extreme, but I remind you that this was the same man who said, "Expect great things from God; attempt great things for God." During his lifetime his work in India included church planting, education, medical relief, Bible translation and production, linguistic and horticultural research, and social reform. This "grain of wheat" was willing to "die," and his life brought forth "much fruit!"

The greatness of a man's power is the measure of his surrender.[6]

—WILLIAM BOOTH,
FOUNDER OF THE SALVATION ARMY

1. List the seven areas of submission.

    _____

    _____

    _____

    _____

    _____

    _____

    _____

2. List the seven scriptural principles of submission.

    _____

    _____

    _____

    _____

    _____

    _____

    _____

A Treacherous Animal

*I count him braver who overcomes
his desires than him who conquers his
enemies, for the hardest victory is victory
over self.[1]*

—ARISTOTLE

SEVERAL YEARS AGO I HAD the privilege to have
a retired veteran minister sit under my ministry. He had
preached longer than I was old. His ministry had been
in the pastorate, and remarkably fruitful. I felt blessed to
have this seasoned minister in my congregation.

We were talking one day about the sadness of disunity
and division in some churches and the way church people
can behave. He then said something that struck a chord
with me that I have never forgotten, "David, human nature
is a treacherous animal!" I know there are some very godly
people in our churches who exemplify Christ; however, it is
also true that this thing called "the flesh" can wreak havoc
in a church, family, friends, and so on. D. L. Moody said,
"God sends no one away empty except those who are full
of themselves." [2] When you truly get tired of being full
of yourself and being robbed of God's best, you'll make a
decision to change. This brings us to another principle of
discipleship, and that is *self-denial and cross-bearing*.

Paul said in Romans 8:8, "So then, those who are in the
flesh cannot please God." By "the flesh" Paul means the old
human nature. This is why self-denial and cross-bearing

is vital to discipleship training. Even though in our day the cross is worn as jewelry and placed on top of church buildings as a positive symbol, this was not true in New Testament culture. In that day it was reserved for the worst criminals. It was an unpopular and shunned object. In 1 Corinthians 1:18 we read, "For the message of the cross is foolishness to those who are perishing." However, there are some life-changing lessons to be learned through our willingness to deny ourselves and take up the cross. I will begin with our Lord, our supreme example.

The true nature of Jesus was that He was both God and man. By being born a human being, he had to be cared for by his parents. As any other child, He had to learn the art of crawling, walking, and talking. In other words, He faced the same limitations as all human beings do, such as exhaustion, thirst, hunger, and so forth. Yet, He was also God, conceived of the Holy Spirit. In Luke 1:35, the angel's words to Mary confirm this: "And the angel answered and said to her, 'The Holy Spirit will come upon you, and the power of the Highest will overshadow you; therefore, also, that Holy One who is to be born will be called the Son of God.'"

These two natures in Jesus posed a conflict. His godly nature easily pleased the Father, but in His human nature He drew back from suffering and pain. We know this to be true because of the incident in the garden. In Luke 22:41–42 we see, "And He was withdrawn from them about a stone's throw, and He knelt down and prayed, saying, 'Father, if it is your will, take this cup away from Me; nevertheless not My will, but yours be done.'" Because Jesus was submitted to His Father's will, He was willing to go to the cross. According to Matthew's account, He could have called to angels to come and deliver Him (Matt. 26:53). Jesus, though, submitted Himself to all the suffering because this was His Father's will. He was willing to do the Father's will no matter the sacrifice, cost, or pain.

It is one thing to talk about Jesus' example, but it is an entirely different thing to follow in His steps. Every one of us, if we are really serious about our walk with the Lord, will ask ourselves some heart-searching questions, questions such as, "What about my own self-denial and my own willingness to deny self?" It is good for us to determine what the words *cost, sacrifice,* and *the cross* mean individually. Centuries ago, Jeanne-Marie Guyon said, "Without crosses, the soul never dies to itself."[3]

If Jesus had never gone to the cross, He would have never experienced the triumph of resurrection. He went to the cross limited by His human body, and He was resurrected in all of His potential. What was true in Jesus' life is true in our lives. In Luke 9:23, Jesus said (to us, too), "If anyone desires to come after Me, let him deny himself, and take up his cross daily, and follow Me." The word *desires* speaks only of those who are sincere. *Deny himself* is for those willing to renounce their selfish will and ways. *Take up his cross daily* means a continual dying to self-will. A cross is something we can either accept or reject. It speaks of our outward expression of what it takes for us to find and do the will of God. It is when His will crosses our will and we choose to submit, no matter the cost or pain. Self-denial is an inner attitude, a commitment, and a decision whereby we say no to self.

In Luke 9:24, Jesus continued and said something that is very hard for us to do because of our two natures: "For whoever desires to save his life will lose it, but whoever loses his life for My sake will save it." What makes this so difficult is our two natures, our self nature and our spiritual nature. Our self nature is our rebellious nature. It is the nature we were born with. It is self-seeking, self-serving, and self-pleasing. For example, no parent ever had to teach their child to be naughty. If you tend to doubt this, put two toddlers in a room with just one toy and see what happens! In Proverbs 22:15, Solomon said, "Foolishness is bound up in the heart of a child." The word *foolishness* speaks of not only mischief, but also of self-will. He says it is "in the heart," meaning an inward inclination to pleasing self. Further, it is "bound," not "found" in them. Some read this, "It is annexed to the heart," speaking of a vicious disposition that cleaves closely to the soul. It may be cute to watch two three-year-olds fight over a toy, but there is nothing funny about watching two adults at the age of forty-three do battle over some "toy" in the church.

I saw a cartoon of two little boys, dirty, ruffled, and scowling at each other while their Sunday school teacher was holding them apart. The pastor is looking at the boys as she states to him, "They were fighting over who made the best angel in the Sunday school play!" In 1 Corinthians 13:11, Paul said, "When I became a man, I put away childish things." The word *things* means "ways." Paul is saying that now that he is an adult, he has put away his childish ways. Believe it or not, the actual meaning of this is that many adults have put away their childhood toys and dolls, but they have never done away with their childish ways of reacting to life. If the flesh is not dealt with, it will grow worse over the years. We do not grow sweet naturally. We must decide to "take it to the cross and deny self!"

Our life is precious to us, and we want things our way, i.e. to "save it" and not to "lose it." We must learn, though, that Christ and self cannot both rule. We cannot have our way and God's way, too. The world may propagate "have it your way" and "the customer is always right," but that does not apply in the kingdom of the Lord Jesus Christ! Our rights are not the priority, but our relationship with our Lord and one another is.

George Mueller, who accomplished remarkable things for the kingdom during the nineteenth century through prayer and faith in God alone, was asked what had been one of the secrets of his life. He answered, "There was a day when I died, utterly died, died to George Mueller and his opinions, preferences, tastes, and will; died to the world, its approval or censure; died to the approval or blame of even my brethren and friends; and since then I have studied only to show myself approved unto God."[4] No wonder his life changed the lives of thousands of orphans in England.

A little girl, seeing a cross on the church communion table, asked, "Mother, what is that plus sign doing on the table?" The cross is God's great plus sign for our lives.

In Luke 14:25–27, 33, Jesus gave us three *cannots*. In verse 26, He says there can be no competition for our love for Christ: "If anyone comes to Me and does not hate [this means to 'love less'] his father and mother, wife and children, brothers and sisters, yes, and his own life also, he *cannot be my disciple.*" In verse 27, He says it must be a life-long commitment: "And whoever does not bear his cross and come after Me *cannot be my disciple.*" Finally, in verse 33, He says there must be a complete surrender: "So likewise, whoever of you does not forsake all that he has *cannot be my disciple.*"

We are an extension of the life and ministry of Christ, and the way He accomplished the Father's purpose is the way we accomplish the Father's purpose—the cross and self-denial.

Hudson Taylor said a Christian should have enough confidence in God to be able to sing the Doxology when scraping the bottom of the barrel. Not long after he made that statement, his own flour barrel was empty and his wife asked him to practice what he preached. He replied, "I will, on one condition—that you put your head in the barrel and sing with me." The two devoted missionaries did, and it's no wonder that God wrought miracles through their ministry![5]

I have been crucified with Christ; it is no longer I who live, but Christ lives in me; and the life which I now live in the flesh I live by faith in the Son of God, who loved me and gave Himself for me.

—Galatians 2:20

1. Take time to think and meditate on the truths of this chapter and write in your words your thoughts and lessons learned:

_____

_____

_____

_____

_____

_____

_____

_____

_____

No One Knows It All

*The beginning of wisdom is silence; the
second stage is listening.*

—HEBREW PROVERB

CHAPTER 12

"TWO MEN WENT TO CHURCH to pray. One was
a so-called leading citizen, and the other was a teacher.
The prominent citizen stood, and with his eyes looking
upward said: 'O Lord, I thank thee that I am not like these
professional men, even as this poor teacher. I pay half the
teacher's salary. It is my money that built this church. I
subscribe liberally to foreign missions and to all the work
of this church. It is my money that advances this cause.'
The teacher's prayer was quite different. He simply bowed
his head in deep humility and said: 'God, be merciful unto
me, I was that man's teacher.'"[1]

Emerson said, "Every man I meet is my master in
some point, and in that I learn of him."[2] This brings
us to another vital principle of discipleship, and that is
teachableness. God wants us all to have a teachable spirit.
However, Scripture declares that a person who is not
teachable is a "fool." This was true of Rehoboam, the son
of Solomon and Naamah, the Ammonitess. Rehoboam
was forty-one years of age when he succeeded his father's
throne and was headstrong and unteachable. First Kings
12:8 says, "But he rejected the advice which the elders had
given him." Verse 15 says, "So the king did not listen."
His arrogant behavior brought division and devastation

to God's people, from which they never recovered. Some-one said, "A wise man changes his mind, a fool never." How true this was of Rehoboam, and the terrible price he paid for being unteachable.

The Bible warns that an unteachable person cannot be taught. Proverbs 1:7 says, "The fear of the LORD is the beginning of knowledge, but fools despise wisdom and instruction." The Hebrew word here for *fool* has strong meaning: "thick, hard, stupid, dull of understanding, con-temptuous trampling under the feet, gross, self-willed and so headstrong they will not hear advice." The word *despise* means, "a condition long continued and still existing." This shows a very serious spiritual problem with some people. Job 11:12 compares an "empty-headed man" to "a wild donkey's colt," which speaks of being stubborn and refusing to obey instruction.

Jesus was teachable. In Luke 2:52, the Scripture states, "And Jesus increased in wisdom and stature, and in favor with God and men." When it says He "increased in wis-dom," literally it means, "He continued to be filled with wis-dom." The idea is of being filled up. It was a process. The Greek tense conveys continued action. Just as Jesus grew physically, He also continued to be filled with wisdom.

Jesus also only taught the teachable. There were four types of people who followed Him. First, the curious: These were the ones who followed Him out of curiosity to see His miracles. Second, the convinced: They believed that He was whom He claimed to be, but their interest took them no further. Third, the committed: These were those who faith-fully followed Him during His life span. Fourth, the con-tinuous: These were those whom He could disciple because they continued in His word. In His parable of the sower, He called them "good soil." In Matthew 13:23, He said, "As for what was sown on good soil, this is he who hears the Word and grasps and comprehends it; he indeed bears fruit and yields in one case a hundred times as much as was sown, in another sixty times as much, and in another thirty" (AMP). In Mark 4:8, we have, "And other seed [of the same kind] fell into good (well-adapted) soil and brought forth grain, growing up and increasing, and yielded up to thirty times as much, and sixty times as much, and even a hundred times as much as had been sown" (AMP). Mark 4:20 says, "And those sown on the good (well-adapted) soil are the ones who hear the Word and receive and accept and welcome it and bear fruit—some thirty times as much as was sown, some sixty times as much, and some [even] a hundred times as much" (AMP). Notice how He has described them in these three verses. They "hear, grasp, and comprehend the Word. They have a well-adapted heart and they receive, accept, and welcome the Word." Jesus invested in the teachable.

The Book of Proverbs admonishes us to receive advice from the wise (Prov. 1:2–7). Wisdom taught here is "skill for living." The word for *wisdom* here is the same word translated *skill* in reference to Bezalel and Aholiab and the detailed work they did in constructing the tabernacle. God gave them skill for carving, building, weaving, and artwork. In Exodus 31:6, God said, "I have put wisdom in the hearts of all." The word for *wisdom* means "cunningness, skill and artistic ability, decision and judgment." This is the fruit of being teachable. You learn "skills for living." Paul told Timothy to "instruct the brethren" (1 Tim. 4:6). The word for *instruct* essentially means "to counsel, to advise, to point out, and to suggest." The connotation does not carry the thought of issuing orders, but of gently offering instruction and giving direction to those who are teachable.

Someone said, "Advice is seldom welcome. Those who need it most like it least." There is a distinct difference between the teachable and the unteachable. According to Scripture, the teachable accept correction and desire to learn and be taught. Thus, they become spiritually mature. However, the unteachable reject correction and instruction. Thus, they remain spiritually immature. Proverbs 10:17 says, "He who keeps instruction is in the way of life, but he who refuses correction goes astray." This verse reveals the causes of direction and misdirection of life. The teachable retain and appreciate ("keeps") instruction. Not only do they have blessing on them in their "way of life," but they also know how to instruct others and lead them in the proper path. The unteachable obstinately refuse instruction and correction because they reveal their faults to them. The result is that they not only "go astray" themselves, but they also lead all who follow them into error. In Proverbs 12:1, we read, "Whoever loves instruction loves knowledge, but he who hates correction is stupid." The Moffat translation states, "He who cares to know, cares to be set right, but he who hates to be admonished is a stupid creature." The word *stupid* means "dumb as a brute beast." Proverbs 13:10 shows us that it is all a matter of humility or pride: "By pride comes nothing but strife, but with the well-advised is wisdom." Pride here speaks of a haughty and overbearing person who is too conceited to receive advice, thus, their life is contentious. However, those who take and follow advice are wise. Proverbs 15:31–32 tells us to be a good listener: "The ear that hears the rebukes of life will abide among the wise. He who disdains instruction despises his own soul, but he who heeds rebuke gets understanding." Here the teachable are on their way to becoming wiser, while the unteachable are committing moral suicide. Then, Proverbs 19:20 speaks of the wisdom of a teachable spirit: "Listen to counsel and receive instruction, that you may be wise in your latter days."

"Long ago, the Native Americans of the Great Plains survived the harsh winters by having grandparents and grandchildren sleep beside each other to keep from freezing to death.

That is a good metaphor for what the generations do for each other. The old need our heat, and we need their light."[3]

> Tell me, I'll forget; show me, I may remember; but involve me, and I'll understand.
>
> —CHINESE PROVERB

1. List the four kinds of people who followed Jesus.

    _____

    _____

    _____

    _____

2. Explain the differences between the teachable and the unteachable from the Scripture references.

    _____

    _____

    _____

    _____

Pillars or Caterpillars?

God does not ask about our ability nor our inability but our availability![1]

—MARY KAY ASH

I READ SOME TIME AGO that a pastor said, "In my church we have two kinds of people: pillars and caterpillars! The pillars support the church, and the caterpillars crawl in and out once a week." Too often we have too many "caterpillars," people like Reuben, the firstborn of Jacob. When his father, Jacob, was aged and nearing death, he called his sons to him and prophesied over each one. What he had to say of his firstborn, Reuben, is quite sad. In Genesis 49:3–4, we read Jacob's words: "Reuben, you are my firstborn, my might and the beginning of my strength, the excellency of dignity and the excellency of power. Unstable as water, you shall not excel." Reuben was a very gifted young man with tremendous potential, but he was "unstable as water," i.e., "reckless, lacked self-control, and not dependable." Thankfully, we have pillars in our churches, too. In Galatians 2:9, Paul wrote of James, Cephas (Peter) and John, calling them "pillars"—men of support and dependability. This introduces an additional principle of discipleship, which is *faithfulness*.

C. H. Spurgeon said, "I know of nothing which I would choose to have as the subject of my ambition for life than to be kept faithful to my God till death."[2] In Galatians 5:22, we find one of the fruits of the Spirit is "faithfulness." Service requires a servant, and servanthood brings faithfulness to mind. In Matthew 25:21, we read, "His lord said to him, 'Well done, good and faithful servant; you were faithful over a few things, I will make you ruler over many things. Enter into the joy of your lord.'" The word used for "faithful" here means, "reliable, to be trusted and loyal." John Wesley averaged preaching three times a day for more than fifty-four years, totaling more than 44,000 times. While doing this, he rode by horseback and carriage more than 200,000 miles, or about 5,000 miles a year. Remember, this was long before modern-day modes of travel. We would have to concur that he was faithful!

Faithfulness is an attribute of God. In Psalm 89:24, 28, 33–34, we find three words linked together when speaking of God's faithfulness—*faithfulness, mercy/loving-kindness,* and *covenant. Faithfulness* speaks of His trustworthiness. *Mercy* and *loving-kindness* are from the same Hebrew word meaning His kindness (grace). *Covenant* speaks of how He keeps His word. It is expressed in verse 24—"But My faithfulness and My mercy shall be with him, and in My name his horn shall be exalted"; verse 28, "My mercy I will keep for him forever, and My covenant shall stand firm with him;" and verses 33–34, "Nevertheless My lovingkindness I will not utterly take from him, nor allow My faithfulness to fail. My covenant I will not break, nor alter the word that has gone out of My lips." In verse 24, His faithfulness and mercy are linked together. In verse 28, His mercy and covenant are linked together. In verses 33 and 34, His loving-kindness and covenant are linked together. Notice that God's faithfulness is based on His covenant commitment (i.e., God keeps His word). God gives and keeps His word, not because we deserve it, but on the basis of His grace (mercy/loving-kindness). On the basis of His grace, He is going to be faithful. His grace (mercy/loving-kindness) is expressed in His faithfulness. He even makes a promise by declaring His promise will "stand firm," nor will He "alter" one word He has spoken. This is what Jeremiah had in mind when he wrote, "Great is Your faithfulness" (Lam. 3:23).

God desires to impart this same nature to us. If God's faithfulness is based on what He says, and what He says is based on His grace, then He wants us to have the same quality—faithfulness. He desires for each of us to be a person of our word, a dependable person. In 2 Timothy 2:2, Paul spoke to Timothy of "faithful men." This is the same word for *faithful* as in Matthew 25:21. The men Paul spoke of were men who were believing, men who were loyal, and men who were reliable. According to his admonishment to Timothy, only these types of people can be discipled. Some students walked up to a man of God as he was working in his garden and asked, "If you knew the Lord would come or you were going to die today, what would you do?" The saint of God smiled and said, "This," and went back to gardening. He had neither fear nor apprehension concerning his future, because he knew he would be found faithful. It is inconsistent for us to claim to be a believer and not be faithful. We are God's children and have the divine nature within us, which is faithfulness. God wants us to be faithful.

Availability, not ability, is of the utmost importance. God expects us to be faithful with the talents he has entrusted to us. The parable of the talents in Matthew 25:14–30 proves this. He also expects us to be faithful even when it costs us. Faithfulness cannot be based on convenience. Our faithfulness must be operative even when it is painful. The psalmist in Psalm 15 gives a descriptive quality of a true believer. In verse 1, we have a question concerning these qualities, and in the remaining verses we have the answers. One answer is found in verse 4: "He who swears to his own hurt and does not change." The New International Version says, "Who keeps his oath even when it hurts." We are to be faithful, even when it is costly and inconvenient.

First John 3:16, says, "By this we know love, because He laid down His life for us. And we also ought to lay down our lives for the brethren." This is talking about God's love in our hearts. It is the kind of love we all need, love that is faithful enough to give of ourselves in faithful service to others. We should be saying to one another, "I will love you, serve you, and defend you, even when it hurts or costs. I am a person you can count on and depend on, because I have given you my word. I will even do for you what you do not deserve." This is the faithfulness of God based on His grace. It is a way of saying, "You can count on me."

Paul emphasized a man's faithfulness, not his ability, achievements, or gifts. Notice how he referred to certain individuals: 1 Corinthians 4:17, "Timothy...my beloved and faithful son in the Lord." Ephesians 6:21, "Tychicus, a beloved brother and faithful minister in the Lord." Colossians 1:7, "Epaphras, our dear fellow servant, who is a faithful minister of Christ."

In Luke 16:10–12, Jesus listed three major areas of faithfulness. First, He said we are to be faithful in small things: "He who is faithful in what is least is faithful also in much; and he who is unjust in what is least is unjust also in much." Missionary Hudson Taylor said, "A little thing is a little thing, but faithfulness to a little thing is a big thing."[3] Jesus grew up knowing He was to be king, yet while He was at home with His parents, He was faithful to them in small things (Luke 2:51–52). David, even after being anointed king, remained faithful in keeping sheep until God's time of fulfillment arrived (1 Sam. 16:11–13, 19). A man once said to John Wesley, "If I could just preach like you, Mr. Wesley, I would be happy and fulfilled." Wesley replied, "My dear brother, we are all building God's temple. Read Nehemiah chapter three and you'll discover that those who repaired the dung gate were just as necessary as those who worked on the fountain gate. Everyone did their part, and you and I can do no more."[4]

Jesus was giving a vital lesson, that those who are faithful in small tasks will prove themselves worthy to be entrusted with larger responsibilities. However, those who treat doing little things with contempt prove themselves unworthy of greater things. I know of a situation where a pastor's wife asked an associate to change a light bulb in the church hallway. He said to her, "I'm the youth pastor. I don't do light bulbs." Not only was this young man insubordinate, but he also robbed himself of further preparation for greater things in the future. Remember, small deeds done are better than great deeds planned.

Second, Jesus said we are to be faithful in finances. He asked, "Therefore if you have not been faithful in the unrighteous mammon, who will commit to your trust the true riches?" (Luke 16:11). David Livingstone said, "I will set no value on anything I have or may possess except in relation to the Kingdom of God."[5] *Mammon* is our money and possessions (Jesus taught more about possessions than He did prayer). According to Christ, our heavenly Father will not trust us with spiritual riches until we can prove our faithfulness in earthly possessions. Until you understand the spiritual principle of faithfulness in possessions, you will never understand the ways and operations of the kingdom of God. We can give without loving, but we cannot love without giving. We cannot be faithful with spiritual riches unless we are faithful with finances. Oswald Chambers said, "The golden rule for understanding in spiritual matters is not intellect, but obedience."[6]

Third, Jesus spoke of being faithful in another man's ministry. He said, "And if you have not been faithful in what is another man's, who will give you what is your own?" (v. 12). You are not qualified to rule until you first learn to serve. You cannot be trusted with your own ministry until you have been a faithful servant under another's ministry. C. H. Spurgeon said, "Every man must serve somebody; we have no choice as to that fact. Those who have no master are slaves to themselves."[7] One reason that some talented and gifted people cannot be effectively used of God is because they are undependable and unfaithful. They only serve when it is to their advantage and convenience. When you can be faithful under another person's ministry, allowing him or her to get all the credit, then God can promote you. Someone asked a famous conductor of a great symphony orchestra which orchestral instrument he considered the most difficult to play. He thought for a moment, then said, "The second fiddle. I can get plenty of first violinists, but to find someone who can play the second fiddle with enthusiasm—that's a problem. And if we have no second fiddle, we have no harmony."

> When eating fruit, think of the person who planted the tree!
>
> —VIETNAMESE PROVERB

1. Three words are linked together when speaking of God's faithfulness. List them.

    _____

    _____

    _____

2. Paul emphasized a man's faithfulness, not his ability, achievements, and gifts. List the Scriptures to prove this.

    _____

    _____

    _____

3. There are three major areas of faithfulness listed by Christ in Luke 16:10–12. List them.

    _____

    _____

    _____

A Medal of Honor

Bulldog believers are trained at "obedience school."[1]

—CHRISTIAN CLIPPINGS

SIR HENRY BRACKENBURY (1837–1914), a military attaché in Paris, was talking to the French statesman Leon Gambetta. Gambetta stated to Brackenbury, "In these days, there are only two things a soldier needs to know. He must know how to march, and he must know how to shoot." Brackenbury, the Englishman, answered back, "I beg your pardon, Excellency, but you have forgotten the most important thing of all!" Gambetta asked, "What's that?" Sir Henry Brackenbury replied, "He must know how to obey!"[2] Oswald Chamber said, "One step forward in obedience is worth years of study about it."[3] This brings us to the next principle of discipleship, which is *obedience to delegated authority.* Samuel said to Saul, "To obey is better than sacrifice" (1 Sam. 15:22). Is there any greater medal of honor to receive than to be known as possessing an obedient heart?

Obedience to God's delegated authority in the church is very important. One reason is because of the two spiritual kingdoms in this world. In Matthew 12:22–28, Jesus spoke of these two kingdoms, God's and Satan's. The kingdom of God is marked by an attitude of love, unity, and submission. In Matthew 26:39, Jesus is the perfect example. He said to His Father, "Not as I will, but as You will."

CHAPTER 14

The kingdom of Satan is marked by an attitude of envy, strife, disloyalty, and rebellion. In Isaiah 14:13–14, he set the example when five times he said, "I will!" Each one of us chooses which kingdom we allow to influence us. When we walk in love, unity, and submission, we are in harmony with the attitude of Christ. When we are disloyal, rebellious, contentious, and envious, we are displaying the spirit of Satan's kingdom.

A second reason obedience to God's delegated authority in the church is important is because of the world in which we live. In Matthew 24:12, Jesus said it would be a world of "lawlessness" greatly lacking in "love." He warned, "And because lawlessness will abound, the love of many will grow cold." The word *lawlessness* means *rebellion. Abound* means "multiply, increase, a large number, throng and populace." The word He used for *love* is the same as found in John 3:16, "the love of God." The spirit of the age is an age of rebellion among the populace and is increasing all the time. Sadly, this same spirit (attitude) has infiltrated our churches! The word for *cold* means "to breathe gently." This speaks of the slow process of deception. As it happens, we are unaware of it. One person has said, "The easiest person to deceive is self." The prophet Hosea said of God's people, "They have dealt treacherously with the LORD" (Hos. 5:7). The phrase *dealt treacherously* means "a bed coverlet." The idea is that the bed may not be clean or may be hiding something, and the viewer may not know it! I have dealt with more than one church person like this. Though rebelliousness, divisiveness, and sowing discord, they were totally unaware of their true heart's condition!

Obedience to God's delegated authority is important because it is a means of dealing with our carnal, rebellious nature. In Matthew 7:17–20, Jesus spoke of two trees. He was actually speaking of two natures. He said, "Even so, every good tree bears good fruit, but a bad tree bears bad fruit. A good tree cannot bear bad fruit, nor can a bad tree bear good fruit. Every tree that does not bear good fruit is cut down and thrown into the fire. Therefore by their fruits you will know them." The good tree speaks of our spiritual nature, and the bad tree speaks of our fleshly nature. Paul, in Galatians 5:17, said that these are contrary to one another. We were born with a rebel nature. Children prove this every day. This nature says, "My way, my things, my rights, etc." Romans 8:8 says this nature "cannot please God." This also supports the truth that we reproduce who we are, not necessarily what we say. Jesus said the good tree (spiritual nature) produces "good fruit," and the bad tree (fleshly nature) produces "bad fruit." This truth is as old as the creation account in Genesis 1. Both plant and animal life reproduce, "according to [their] kind." What is true of them is true of us.

In Matthew 3:10, God gave the answer to this fleshly nature (bad tree): "And even now the ax is laid to the root of the trees. Therefore every tree which does not bear good fruit is cut down and thrown into the fire." The roots must be uprooted! Cutting the branches off the bad tree will not solve the problem. Likewise, our attempt to conceal our rebellion with religious ways will fail. We will eventually be challenged with a correction or reprimand from those over us in the Lord, and resistance will erupt. In Psalm 55:21, David spoke of this very thing. He speaks of those he thought were supportive, but when the occasion arose, he found out differently. He said of them, "The words of his mouth were smoother than butter, but war was in his heart; his words were softer than oil, yet they were drawn swords." Our self-life must be put to death. What we rebelliously want, think, or feel must be denied. The ax (cross) must be applied.

In Romans 8:13, Paul warned, "For if you live according to the flesh, you will die; but if by the Spirit you put to death the deeds of the body, you will live." Again, in Galatians 5:24, he said, "And those who are Christ's have crucified the flesh with its passions and desires." Francis Schaeffer, in his book *A Christian Manifesto*, quotes William Penn concerning the United States: "If we are not ruled by God, then we will be ruled by tyrants."[4] This truth is applicable in the spiritual realm. If we do not crucify and put to death our carnal nature, we will be ruled by the tyrant of self.

Christ Jesus delegates authority to men, and He rules and guides through them. A beggar sat at the gate of a rich man. Every day the benevolent rich man made sure that the poor beggar was well cared for and continually gave gifts to him. One day, the rich man needed to send a message as quickly as possible. Since all his servants were busy, he asked the beggar to make the delivery for him. Lifting himself up with pride, the beggar answered his benefactor with these astonishing words, "I solicit alms, sir, but I do not run errands." How typical of so many, never willing to serve, but only wanting to be served. According to Hebrews 13:7, 17, Christ directs His people through "God-given" leadership. He has also qualified the type of leadership He uses to guide us. Christ's leadership will give us the Word of God. Its example will be one of Christlikeness. It will have a deep concern for our spiritual health, and its leadership will have eternity in view. It is to these type leaders only we are to be obedient.

God nowhere expects us to obey someone on an ego trip, seeking to control and manipulate us. Paul told Timothy that the relationship between the pastor and the church is like that of a father and son. In 1 Timothy 3:5, he compared a person's leadership in the church to that of the home when he wrote, "For if a man does not know how to rule his own house, how will he take care of the church of God?" Paul was Timothy's spiritual father. In 1 Timothy 1:2 and 2 Timothy 1:2, Paul called Timothy "a beloved son" and "my son." The church should have the same security with its leadership as a family has with a godly father. Then we are to demonstrate the same respect and appreciation toward our "under-shepherds" as we would give our earthly father.

Our relationship to Christ's delegated authority is reflected in our relationship to Christ. We cannot treat God's leadership one way and Christ another way. We are to receive Christ. We are to receive whom He sends. In Luke 10:16, Jesus said to the seventy as He sent them out, "He who hears you hears Me, he who rejects you rejects Me, and he who rejects Me, rejects Him who sent Me." He said to the twelve, "Most assuredly, I say to you, he who receives whomever I send receives Me; and he who receives Me receives Him who sent Me" (John 13:20).

A little boy was told by his father that he had to go someplace. The boy said, "I ain't go'in." The dad didn't like that kind of language and said, "Now, son, you're not supposed to use the word 'ain't'. That's not proper English." So he gave him a little English lesson:

1. First person singular—"I am not going."
2. Second person singular—"You are not going."
3. Third person singular—"He is not going."
4. First person plural—"We are not going."
5. Second person plural—"You are not going."
6. Third person plural—"They are not going."

The dad then asked, "Son, do you understand it?" The son answered, "Yeah, sounds like to me there ain't nobody go'in."

God gives direction and guidance through His delegated leadership. If we are going to make progress, we must walk in obedience to them, as unto the Lord.

> We are channels through which God's will can flow. If the channels are clogged with our own wills—conceits, prejudices, unworthy ambitions—how can we be used of God?[5]

91

1. List the two spiritual kingdoms operating in today's world.

   _____

   _____

   _____

   _____

2. Explain what you have learned from Matthew 3:10.

   _____

   _____

   _____

   _____

3. What does Hebrews 13:7, 17 mean to you?

   _____

   _____

   _____

   _____

A Polished Shaft

*I used to ask God if He would come and
help me; then I asked God if I might come
and help Him; then I ended by asking
Him to do His own work through me.* [1]

—HUDSON TAYLOR

IN ISAIAH 49:2, THE PROPHET said, "And he has
made my mouth like a sharp sword; in the shadow of His
hand He has hidden me, and made me a polished shaft; in
His quiver He has hidden me." This verse found its perfect fulfillment in the promised Messiah. In a secondary
sense, it applied also to Isaiah. However, it also applies to
what God desires to do in us. This brings us to the final
principle of discipleship, *released for our own ministry.* God
wants to make our "mouth like a sharp sword." The sword
is not for the sharpness of cutting and wounding words,
but for words of effectiveness. The Bible says of Stephen,
"And they were not able to resist the wisdom and the Spirit
by which he spoke" (Acts 6:10).

God also has another purpose, and that is to make us
"a polished shaft." This speaks of the shaft of an arrow
or spear. The wood used by arrow makers for shafts was
extraordinarily crooked at first. They would strip off all
leaves and twigs, and then place it in the fire, careful not
to kindle it, but to make it very hot. They would force it
between two rows of pegs into the ground in a straight line,
an inch or two apart. After cooling, it would be removed,

not quite as crooked as before. This process would be repeated as many times as it took to make the shaft straight. When it was straight, a knife would be used to remove any remaining projections where thorns or branches had been. A powdered potsherd and an old skin were then used as sandpaper to polish the rod to near perfect smoothness. Oil was then used to polish. Even though prepared, the hunter or soldier would then place (hide) it in his quiver until the opportune time. This is the process God uses to make us effective for His purposes. It is usually a very trying time, when all polished and ready for use, to be concealed in His quiver. Solomon wrote in Proverbs 3:11–12, "My son, do not despise the chastening of the Lord, nor detest His correction. For whom the LORD loves He corrects, just as a father the son in whom he delights." And Hebrews 12:11 reminds us, "Now no chastening seems to be joyful for the present, but painful; nevertheless, afterward it yields the peaceable fruit of righteousness to those who have been trained by it."

God has His time of release. He hid Joseph. In Psalm 105:19–22, we read of Joseph, "Until the time that his word came to pass, the word of the LORD tested him. The king sent and released him, the ruler of the people let him go free. He made him lord of his house, and ruler of all his possessions, to bind his princes at his pleasure, and teach his elders wisdom." God hid Moses. The same psalm says of Moses, when his time had come, "He sent Moses unto them." God hid John the Baptist. In Luke 1:80, Luke says of him, "So the child grew and became strong in spirit, and was in the deserts till the day of his manifestation to Israel." Luke 3:2 adds, "The word of God came to John the son of Zacharias in the wilderness." Before his release by his God, John was becoming "strong in spirit," and "the Word of God" was coming to him. His words were then "like a sharp sword," for he demanded, "Make straight the way of the Lord" (John 1:23). Furthermore, he knew more about the heart and purposes of God than the entire religious establishment in Jerusalem. While they were blind to the manifestation of God through Jesus Christ, it took John to recognize and declare, "Behold the Lamb of God!" (John 1:36). A phrase in Hamlet states, "There's a divinity that shapes our ends."[2] It is just as true of us as it was with Christ and the twelve disciples. Mark summarizes His process with them, "Then He appointed twelve, that they might be with Him and that He might send them out to preach." First, they had to be with Him, which was the straightening and polishing process; then He released them.

Three principles are involved in order to be released for ministry. First, we are released after working under supervision. This was the pattern for Timothy. He was a son of a Greek father and a Jewish mother and was destined to be used of God. However, he worked under Paul's supervision before he had his own ministry. In 1 Timothy 1:2, on Paul's first missionary journey, he called him, with great affection, "a true son in the faith." Timothy's name means "honored of God" or "valued of God." He became a pastor in his own right, receiving two pastoral letters from Paul, 1 and 2 Timothy. This is just the point in Luke 16:12, where Jesus taught that if you will be faithful under another's supervision and ministry, one day you will be released for your own.

Second, we are released to make assignments after we have demonstrated a willingness to follow assignments. Charles Haddon Spurgeon said, "It needs more skill than I can tell, to play the second fiddle well."[3] Jesus taught in Luke 16:10 that if we are faithful in small things, God will entrust us with greater things.

Third, we are released after prayerful recognition by the leaders. Proverbs 27:2 states, "Let another man praise you, and not your own mouth." This was the pattern in the Book of Acts. In Acts 13:1–4, it was the recognition of the leadership that resulted in sending out Barnabas and Saul (Paul).

Recognition comes after demonstrating a willingness to be a servant. In 1 Kings 19:21, the Bible says of Elisha, "Then he arose and followed Elijah, and became his servant." The word for *servant* means, "to wait on, serve, do menial tasks." Elisha did this for six years. After Elijah was translated, he became chief prophet in the northern kingdom and had a ministry that lasted for fifty-five years.

In Luke 22:24–27, Jesus described the path to leadership. The disciples were disputing over which one of them was the greatest. (Sound familiar?) He answered, "The kings of the Gentiles exercise lordship over them, and those who exercise authority over them are called 'benefactors.' But not so among you; on the contrary, he who is greatest among you, let him be as the younger, and he who governs as he who serves" (vv. 25–27).

Hudson Taylor said, "When God wants to do His great works, He trains somebody to be quiet enough and little enough, then He uses that person."[4] Before God will allow you to lead, He will develop in you a servant's heart. He is more concerned about the worker than the work, people than programs, building character than churches, the depth of your life than the breadth of your ministry, spiritual quality than numerical quantity, a submissive attitude than a sensational ministry, your relationship with your family and friends than the report of your ministry, priorities than performances, grace than gifts.

Recognition comes when you demonstrate commitment. You must learn to be committed: first, to God, then to your local church and fellow believers. Further, recognition comes when you demonstrate submission. Your submission is tested only when it requires you to do something you would not otherwise do, or do not want to do. If you are asked to do something, your submission will cause you to do it. Submission is an attitude; obedience is conduct. A rebel seeks to find fault with the authority over him so he will have an excuse for not submitting. Remember, we first prove ourselves faithful and efficient in our assignments before we are qualified to have greater areas of service. Become "a polished shaft," and in God's timing, He will release you.

The following words were written on the tomb of an Anglican bishop in the crypts of Westminster Abbey: "When I was young and free and my imagination had no limits, I dreamed of changing the world. As I grew older and wiser, I discovered the world would not change, so I shortened my sights somewhat and decided to change only my country. But it, too, seemed immovable. As I grew into my twilight years, in one last desperate attempt, I settled for changing only my family, those closest to me, but alas, they would have none of it. And now as I lie on my deathbed, I suddenly realize if I had only changed myself first, then by example I would have changed my family. From their inspiration and encouragement, I would then have been able to better my country and, who knows, I may have even changed the world."[5]

Diamonds are chunks of coal that stuck to their job.[6]
—*Bulletin Digest*

1. We are released for ministry based on three principles.
    List them.

    _____

    _____

    _____

    _____

2. Complete the following statement: Before God will
    allow you to lead, He will develop in you a servant's
    heart. He is more concerned about:

    _____

    _____

    _____

    _____

The Commitment of the Christian Leader

I'M A PART OF THE fellowship of the unashamed. I have Holy Spirit power. The die has been cast; I have stepped over the line. The decision has been made. I'm a disciple of His. I won't look back, let up, slow down, back away, or be still. My past is redeemed, my present makes sense, and my future is secure. I'm finished and done with low living, sight walking, small planning, smooth knees, colorless dreams, tamed visions, mundane talking, cheap giving, and dwarfed goals. I no longer need preeminence, prosperity, position, promotions, plaudits, or popularity. I don't have to be right, first, tops, recognized, praised, or rewarded. I now live by faith, lean on His presence, walk by patience, lifted by prayer, and labor by power. My face is set, my gait is fast, my goal is heaven, my road is narrow, my way is rough, my companions few, my guide reliable, and my mission clear. I cannot be bought, compromised, detoured, lured away, turned back, deluded, or delayed. I will not flinch in the face of sacrifice, hesitate in the presence of the adversary, negotiate at the table of the enemy, ponder at the pool of popularity, or meander in the maze of mediocrity. I won't give up, shut up, or let up until I have stayed up, stored up, prayed up, paid up, and preached up for the cause of Christ. I am a disciple of Jesus. I must go 'til He comes, give 'til I drop, preach 'til all know, and work 'til He stops me. And when He comes for His own, He will have no problem recognizing me—my banner will be clear![1]

Notes

Chapter 1
Choice, Not Chance, Determines Destiny

1. Dietrich Bonhoeffer, *The Cost of Discipleship* (New York: Touchstone, 1959), 11.

2. Source obtained from the Internet at http://www. heroesofhistory.com/page69.html (accessed 11/10/05).

3. Billy Graham, *Till Armageddon* (Waco, TX: Word Books, 1981), 198.

4. Source obtained from the Internet at http://psalm121. ca/quotes/dcqarchive0905.html (accessed November 6, 2005).

5. Source obtained from the Internet at http:// plymouthbrethren.org/page.asp?page_id=545 (accessed November 9, 2005).

Chapter 2
The Generals Only?

1. Source obtained from the Internet at http:// en.thinkexist.com/quotes/johnwesley (accessed November 8, 2005).

2. Source obtained from the Internet at http://print. google.com/print?q=sharpshooters+in+the+battle+of+new+ orleans+&oi=print (accessed November 9, 2005).

3. Michael P. Green, *Illustrations for Biblical Preaching* (Grand Rapids: Baker, 1989), 216.

3. Bonhoeffer, *The Cost of Discipleship*, 59.

Chapter 3
A Valuable Pearl

1. B. H. Clendennen, *Restoring the Message of Pentecost* (Beaumont, TX: Voice of Victory Temple, 1990), 99.

2. B. H. Clendennen, *The Holy Spirit* in The School of Christ Series (Beaumont, TX: Voice of Victory, 1992), lesson #11, p. 1.

3. Source obtained from the Internet at www. brainyquote.com (accessed July 7, 2005).

4. Eugene Myers Harrison, "John Geddie, 1815–1872, Messenger of the Love of Christ in Eastern Melanesia," Worldwide Missions Missionary Biographies, http://www.wholesomewords.org/missions/biogeddie.html (accessed November 6, 2005).

6. Dave Breese, "Breathless With Anticipation," *Destiny Newsletter,* http://christiandestiny.org/publications/newsletter/2004-07/thinking-together.shtml (accessed November 8, 2005).

Chapter 4
Those Who See the Invisible Can Do the Impossible

1. Source obtained from the Internet at http://www.crossroad.to/Excerpts/books/faith/tozer-quotes.htm (accessed November 8, 2005).

2. Source obtained from the Internet at http://www.ecotopia.org/ehof/thoreau/bio.html (accessed November 6, 2005).

3. Source obtained from the Internet at http://www.tscpulpitseries.org/english/undated/tsglory.html (accessed November 8, 2005).

4. Leonard Ravenhill, *America Is Too Young to Die* (Minneapolis, MN: Bethany House Publishers, 1979), 82–83.

5. "Saint Joan by George Bernard Shaw," http://faculty.smu.edu/bwheeler/Joan_of_Arc/crshaw.pdf (accessed July 7, 2005).

5. Brainy Quote, Ferdinand Foch Quotes, http://www.brainyquote.com/quotes/authors/f/ferdinand_foch.html

(accessed July 7, 2005).

6. Source obtained from the Internet at http://www.dailybread.org.uk/pda/051121x.rtf (accessed November 9, 2005).

Chapter 5
Seeing Eye to Eye and Walking Arm in Arm

1. *Our Daily Bread* (Grand Rapids, MI: RBC Ministries, May/June 1996), 1.

2. *Webster's New World Dictionary of the American Language*, College Edition (New York: The World Publishing Co., 1966).

3. *Our Daily Bread* (Grand Rapids, MI: RBC Ministries, June–August), 14.

Chapter 6
A Revolution

1. *Today's Pentecostal Evangel* (Springfield, MO: Gospel Publishing House, April 8, 2001).

2. Robert H. Schuller, *Discover Your Possibilities* (New York: Ballantine Books, 1986), 160.

3. Source obtained from the Internet at http://www.wholesomewords.org/missions/giants/biolivingstone.html (accessed November 7, 2005).

4. Vance Havner, *Road to Revival* (Westwood, NJ: Fleming H. Revell Co., 1940), 84.

5. Source obtained from the Internet at http://www.bible.org/illus.asp?topic_id=414 (accessed November 8, 2005).

Chapter 7
It Is Not What, but Who

1. Billy Graham, *Till Armageddon* (Nashville, TN: Word

Books, 1981), 187.

    2. William Barclay, *The Letters to Timothy, Titus, and Philemon* (Louisville, KY: Westminster John Knox Press, 1975), 254–255.

    3. *Today's Pentecostal Evangel*, (Springfield, MO: Gospel Publishing House, April 8, 2001).

    4. Source obtained from the Internet at http://www.wholesomewords.org/missions/giants/biolivingstone.html (accessed November 7, 2005).

    4. Robert E. Coleman, *The Coming World Revival* (Wheaton, IL: Crossway Books, 1995), 83.

Chapter 8
'Til Death Do Us Part

    1. Source obtained from the Internet at http://chi.gospelcom.net/DAILYF/2003/11/daily-11-17-2003.shtml (accessed November 7, 2005).

    2. Source obtained from the Internet at http://en.thinkexist.com/quotes/johnwesley (accessed November 7, 2005).

    3. Source obtained from the Internet at http://www.brainyquote.com/quotes/h/henrifrede148217.html (accessed November 9, 2005).

    4. Basil Miller, *John Wesley* (Minneapolis, MN: Bethany House, 1943), 91.

    5. Leonard Ravenhill, *America Is Too Young to Die* (Minneapolis, MN: Bethany Fellowship, 1979), 64–65.

Chapter 9
A Vertical Relationship

    1. Source obtained from the Internet at http://www.pietyhilldesign.com/gcq/quotepages/creation.html (accessed November 7, 2005).

    1 *Our Daily Bread* (Grand Rapids, MI: RBC Ministries,

June–August, 2002), August 7.

2. Source obtained from the Internet at http://home.neo.rr.com/monroe/990307a.htm (accessed November 8, 2005).

Chapter 10
Horizontal Results

1. *Our Daily Bread* (Grand Rapids, MI: RBC Ministries, January/February 1996).

2. "Pascal's Vision," quoted at http://justus.anglican.org/resources/bio/233.html (accessed November 7, 2005).

3. Source obtained from the Internet at http://www.longang.com/exlibris/misc/1536-jc.htm (accessed November 6, 2005).

4. *Pulpit Helps* (Chattanooga, TN: AMG International, March 1997).

5. Source obtained from the Internet at http://www.sbcommunity.org/news/cn0804pg1.asp (accessed November 7, 2005).

6. Source obtained from the Internet at http://en.thinkexist.com/quotes/william booth (accessed November 8, 2005).

Chapter 11
A Treacherous Animal

1. Source obtained from the Internet at http://www.quotationspage.com/quote/29862.html (accessed November 9, 2005).

2. Source obtained from the Internet at http://www.wholesomewords.org/devotion1.html (accessed November 8, 2005).

3. *Pulpit Helps* (Chattanooga, TN: AMG International, May 2004), 16.

4. Source obtained from the Internet at http://www.whatsaiththescripture.com/voice/george.mueller.of.Bristol.24.

html (accessed November 7, 2005).

5. *The Sunshine Bulletin* (Lakeland, FL: Peninsular Florida District Council of the Assemblies of God, November 1972).

Chapter 12
No One Knows It All

1. *Christian Clippings* (New Port Richey, FL: February 1997).
2. Source obtained from the Internet at http://www. Kettering.edu/%7Ejhuggins/humor/quotes.html (accessed November 7, 2005).
3. Dr. Mary Pipher, "Another Country," *Readers Digest*, October 2000.

Chapter 13
Pillars or Caterpillars?

1. Source obtained from the Internet at http://www. fidnet.com~suebrown/keepers.html (accessed November 6, 2005).
2. Source obtained from the Internet at http://www. biblebb.com/files/spurgeon/0554.htm (accessed November 7, 2005).
3. Source obtained from the Internet at http://www. mypasture.org/narrow.htm (accessed November 7, 2005).
4. Dave Sutherland and Kirk Nowery, *The 33 Laws of Stewardship* (Camarillo, CA: Spire Resources, 2003), 69.
5. Source obtained from the Internet at http://www. wholesomewords.org/missions/bliving2.html (accessed November 7, 2005).
6. *Today's Pentecostal Evangel* (Springfield, MO: Gospel Publishing House, April 15, 2001)
7. Source obtained from the Internet at http://www. biblestudyplanet.com/good2.htm (accessed November 7, 2005).

Chapter 14
A Medal of Honor

1. *Christian Clippings* (New Port Richey, FL: February 1999).

2. Louis Albert Banks, "Fresh Bait for Fishers of Men," http://www.freshministry.org/021300.html (accessed November 7, 2005).

3. *Our Daily Bread* (Grand Rapids, MI: RBC Ministries, March 4, 1993).

4. Francis Schaeffer, *A Christian Manifesto* (Westchester, IL: Crossway Books, 1981), 34.

5. "Advance," *Presbyterian Survey*, July 8, 1973.

Chapter 15
A Polished Shaft

1. Source obtained from the Internet at http://www.higherpraise.com/illustrations/availability.htm (accessed November 7, 2005).

2. William Shakespeare, "The Tragedy of Hamlet," http://users.rcn.com/spiel/hamletb.html (accessed November 7, 2005).

3. Source obtained from the Internet at http://www.kovess.com/newsletter.asp?offset=10ItemNo=145 (accessed November 6, 2005).

4. Source obtained from the Internet at http://www.rdcministries.homestead.com/xmas2001.html (accessed November 7, 2005).

5. Source obtained from the Internet at http://unsolved-mysteries.com/usm393844.html (accessed November 7, 2005).

6. *Pulpit Helps* (Chattanooga, TN: AMG International, October 2003).

Conclusion

1. Bob Moorhead, "The Commitment of the Christian Leader," *Pulpit Helps* 9, no. 1.

To Contact the Author

To order additional copies of *Discipleship Manual*:

www.davidarnoldonline.org

or phone toll free:

1-866-396-READ

To contact Dave Arnold by E-mail:

davidarnold1@verizon.net